THE ROYAL COURT THEATRE PRESENT

Blue Mist

by Mohamed-Zain Dada

Blue Mist was first performed at the Royal Court Jerwood Theatre
Upstairs, Sloane Square, on Thursday 5 October 2023.

Blue Mist

by Mohamed-Zain Dada

Cast (in alphabetical order)

Asif **Salman Akhtar**
Jihad **Omar Bynon**
Rashid **Arian Nik**

Director **Milli Bhatia**
Designer **Tomás Palmer**
Lighting Designer **Elliot Griggs**
Sound Designer **Elena Peña**
Movement Director **Theophilus O. Bailey**
Production Manager **Tabitha Piggott**
Stage Managers **Catriona McHugh & Charlotte Padgham**
Lighting Programmer **Jodie Underwood**
Costume Supervisor **Isabelle Cook**
Hair Stylist **Jess Radice**
Outreach Coordinator **Hannah Ali**
Artist Wellbeing Practitioner **Lou Platt**

From the Royal Court, on this production:

Casting Directors **Amy Ball & Arthur Carrington**
Stage Supervisors **TJ Chappell-Meade & Steve Evans**
Lead Producer **Jasmyn Fisher-Ryner**
Sound Supervisor **David McSeveney**
Costume Supervisors **Katie Price & Lucy Walshaw**
Company Manager **Mica Taylor**
Lighting Supervisor **Deanna Towli**

Blue Mist is a co-production with SISTER.

The Royal Court Theatre and Stage Management wish to thank the following for their help with this production:
Sanjeev Bhaskar (Voice of Chunky), Kali Claire (Vocal Support), Matt Curr, Zainab Hasan, Lauren Patman, Sunspel,
Centreline Fabrications (Ceiling Build), Propworks (Hookah Pipe).

Mohamed-Zain Dada (Writer)

As writer, for the Royal Court: **SW1: Loot, Living Newspaper: Emily (Glitched) in Paris.**

As writer, other theatre includes: **Zidane of the Ends (High Tide).**

As director, theatre includes: **The End of Diaspora (Free Word Centre).**

Film includes: **Otherstani, The Moon is a Meme.**

Salman Akhtar (Asif)

Theatre includes: **Tartuffe (& Birmingham Rep), Timon of Athens, Tamburlaine (RSC); Platform (Old Vic New Voices); The Flood (Young Vic).**

Television includes: **Man like Mobeen Series 1 & 4, Andor, Finding Alice, Doctors, Three Girls, Murdered by My Father, Parents of the Band.**

Milli Bhatia (Director)

As director, for the Royal Court: **Baghdaddy, Maryland, seven methods of killing kylie jenner, Living Newspaper, My White Best Friend (and Other Letters Left Unsaid), This Liquid Earth: A Eulogy in Verse (Edinburgh International Festival), Half Full (& RWCMD), Dismantle This Room.**

As assistant director, for the Royal Court: **Inside Bitch (& Clean Break), Poet in da Corner, One For Sorrow, Instructions for Correct Assembly, Girls & Boys.**

As director, other theatre includes: **Chasing Hares (Young Vic); seven methods of killing kylie jenner (Riksteatern, Stadsteatern, Dramaten (Scenkonstbiennalen), The Public Theater NY, Woolly Mammoth DC); Dismantle This Room, The Hijabi Monologues (Bush); My White Best Friend (and Other Letters Left Unsaid) (Bunker); I'm Tired Of Waiting, Someone Pass Me The Duct Tape, (Stratford East).**

As director, film includes: **The Magic Finger (Roald Dahl Story Company/Unicorn); seven methods of killing kylie jenner, Living Newspaper (Royal Court); HOME(BODY) or The Tall Story (Young Vic); Tiny Dancers (NYT); Yash Gill's Power Half Hour.**

As director, radio includes: **Ghosts In The Blood (Audible).**

Omar Bynon (Jihad)

Omar is an actor, writer and workshop facilitator from East London.

Theatre includes: **Duck (Arcola); Julius Caesar (Globe); 2036: Pawn (Bush); Heartfelt, Poet's Manifesto (Stratford East); King Lear, The Oresteia, A Bold Stroke for a Wife, Julius Caesar, Mysterious Bruises, The Laramie Project, The Importance of Being Earnest (RADA).**

Theophilus O. Bailey (Movement Director)

Theophilus is a movement director, choreographer, dancer and actor.

For the Royal Court: **For Black Boys Who Have Considered Suicide When The Hue Gets Too Heavy (& West End).**

As assistant choreographer, theatre includes: **See Us (Royal Opera House).**

As dancer, theatre includes: **Blak Whyte Gray (Barbican); Born to Manifest (Curve).**

As actor and dancer, film includes: **Magic Mike's Last Dance, Here/Not Here.**

Isabelle Cook (Costume Supervisor)

As design assistant/buyer, television includes: **Queen Charlotte: A Bridgerton Story.**

As crowd costume assistant, television includes: **Gangs of London.**

As principal standby, television includes: **Mary and George.**

As costume designer, film includes: **Hermit, Measure, Sensory Prosthetics, In Vitro.**

As key crowd, film includes: **People We Hate At The Wedding.**

As crowd standby, film and television includes: **The Three-Body Problem, I Hate Suzie, Ted Lasso, SAS Rogue Heroes, Damsel, Snow White, Bridgerton.**

Elliot Griggs (Lighting Designer)

For the Royal Court: **all of it, A Fight Against...
(Una Lucha Contra...), Purple Snowflakes and
Titty Wanks (& Abbey Theatre, Dublin), Living
Newspaper, On Bear Ridge (& National Theatre
Wales), Yen (& Royal Exchange, Manchester).**

Other theatre includes: **Jitney (Old Vic/Leeds
Playhouse/Headlong); Amélie the Musical (The
Other Palace/Watermill/ West End/UK Tour);
Fleabag (Soho/ Edinburgh Fringe Festival/West
End/SoHo Playhouse, NYC/Tour); The Wild Duck
(Almeida); The Lover/The Collection (West
End); An Octoroon (& Orange Tree), Pomona
(& Royal Exchange/Orange Tree) (National);
Beautiful Thing (Stratford East); No Pay? No
Way!, Queens of the Coal Age, The Night Watch
(Royal Exchange, Manchester); Sleepova, The P
Word, Hir (Bush); The Swell, The Misfortune of
the English, Last Easter, The Sugar Syndrome,
Low Level Panic, Sheppey, buckets (Orange
Tree); Missing Julie (Theatr Clwyd); Ivan &
the Dogs (Young Vic); Richard III (Headlong);
Disco Pigs (Trafalgar Studios 2/Irish Rep,
NYC); Acceptance, Dry Powder, Diminished
(Hampstead); Feeling Afraid As If Something
Terrible Is Going To Happen (Roundabout);
Psychodrama (Traverse); Blue Door (Ustinov);
Loot (Park/Watermill); The Trial of Josie K
(Unicorn); Fool For Love (Found111); The Oracles
(Punchdrunk); Martha, Josie & the Chinese
Elvis (& Octagon), Educating Rita (Hull Truck);
Shift, Bromance (Barely Methodical Troupe).**

Live events include: **I Sea You (World Economic
Forum), Lost Lagoon, Height of Winter, The
Single-Opticon, Alcoholic Architecture
(Bompas & Parr).**

Awards include: **Off West End Award for Best
Lighting Designer (Pomona), Olivier Award
for Outstanding Achievement in an Affiliate
Theatre (The P Word), Roundabout. Fringe First
Award (Feeling Afraid As If Something Terrible
Is Going To Happen).**

Catriona McHugh
(Stage Manager - Props)

Theatre includes: **Oklahoma! (West End); Who
Killed My Father (Young Vic); NW Trilogy (Kiln);
Albion, Three Sisters, The Writer, The Twilight
Zone (Almeida); Unknown Rivers (Hampstead);
Anna Bella Eema, Hoard (Arcola); Chasing Bono
(Soho); Wasted (Southwark).**

Awards include: **Olivier Award for Best Musical
Revival (Oklahoma!)**

Arian Nik (Rashid)

For the Royal Court: **Sokhan Begoo.**

Other theatre includes: **Kabul Goes Pop: Music
Television Afghanistan (Hightide/Brixton
House); Pufferfish (VAULT Festival); The Village
(Stratford East); The Last Testament of Lillian
Bocca (Hull Truck); The Ugly One (Park).**

Television includes: **Passenger, Count Abdulla,
Bruce, The Bay, Ackley Bridge, Killing Eve.**

Film includes: **Allelujah, The Bower, Dating Amber,
Artemis Fowl, The Beekeeper.**

Radio includes: **Hal, Doctor Who: Absolute Power.**

Charlotte Padgham
(Stage Manager - On Book)

For the Royal Court: **all of it (Festival
d'Avignon/2023/2020), Baghdaddy, Living
Archive, For Black Boys Who Have Considered
Suicide When The Hue Gets Too Heavy [job
share], Rare Earth Mettle, Living Newspaper,
Midnight Movie, Cyprus Avenue, ear for eye,
Girls & Boys, a profoundly affectionate,
passionate devotion to someone (-noun), hang,
Posh (& West End), truth and reconciliation,
Catch, On Insomnia and Midnight, The
Winterling, My Name is Rachel Corrie (& West
End), Fireface, The Force of Change, Dublin
Carol.**

Other theatre includes: **The Dry House (Marylebone
Theatre); Hamlet, King Lear (Globe); Life of
Galileo (Young Vic); Complicit, Speed-the-Plow,
All About My Mother, The Entertainer (Old
Vic); Aristocrats, Appropriate, Fathers and
Sons (Donmar); Chimerica (& West End), Game
(Almeida); The Invisible Hand, The House That
Will Not Stand, Red Velvet(& NY), The Bomb: a
partial history, The Riots, Tactical Questioning,
Greta Garbo Came to Donegal (Kiln); Shopping
and F***ing, Herons, Tipping the Velvet (Lyric
Hammersmith); nut (National).**

Charlotte has also worked at Trafalgar
Studios, The Gate, Soho and Hampstead
theatres, and for The Philip Lawrence Awards,
Shared Experience and Les Enfants Terribles.
She has been a visiting professional, assessor
& mentor to stage management students at
the Royal Central School of Speech and Drama
since 2006.

Tomás Palmer (Designer)

As associate designer, for the Royal Court: **Sound of the Underground.**

Other theatre includes: **The Bacchae (Lyric Hammersmith); Julius Caesar [co-costume design with Rosanna Vize] (RSC); My Uncle Is Not Pablo Escobar (Brixton House); Sanctuary (Access All Areas); Sophocles' Oedipus/Silent Practice (LAMDA); The Wellspring [co-design with Rosie Elnile] (Royal & Derngate); Time Is Running Out (Gate Cardiff); Half Full (RWCMD); Winning (Glasgow School of Art); Autocue (Centre for Contemporary Art Glasgow).**

As associate designer, other theatre includes: **The Cherry Orchard (Yard/ETT/HOME).**
As production designer, film includes: **Too Rough.**

Elena Peña (Sound Designer)

For the Royal Court: **Baghdaddy, two Palestinians go dogging, seven methods of killing kylie jenner, Maryland, Living Newspaper.**

Other theatre includes: **As You Like It (RSC); Wuthering Heights (China Plate/UK Tour); Misty (Shed NYC); Silence (Donmar/Tara); The Chairs (Almeida); seven methods of killing kylie jenner (Riksteatern, Sweden/Public Theater NYC); The Darkest Part of The Night, Reasons (You Shouldn't Love Me), Snowflake (Kiln); Nora: A Doll's House, Macbeth, Mountains (Royal Exchange); Rockets And Blue Lights (& Royal Exchange), Trouble In Mind, Brainstorm (& Company3) (National); The Memory of Water (Nottingham Playhouse); The Remains of the Day (Royal and Derngate); Autoreverse (BAC); Misty (& West End), Going Through, HIR, Islands (Bush); Thick As Thieves (Clean Break); Double Vision (Wales Millennium Centre); The Caretaker (Bristol Old Vic); The Lounge (Soho/Summer Hall, Edinburgh/Riksteatern, Sweden); The Bear/The Proposal, Flashes (Young Vic); Sleepless (Analogue/Staatstheater Mainz, Germany).**

Dance includes: **Patrias, Quimeras (Sadlers Wells/Paco Peña Flamenco Company).**

Television/digital includes: **Hope (Clean Break); Have Your Circumstances Changed?, Brainstorm, The Astro Science Challenge, Women of Troy.**

Radio/digital includes: **The Meet Cute, Twelve Years, Duchamps' Urinal (BBC Radio 4); Rockets and Blue Lights (BBC Radio 3); All Of Me (Caroline Horton); Rockpool (Inspector Sands).**
Installation includes: **Have Your Circumstances Changed?, Yes, These Eyes Are The Windows (Artangel).**

Tabitha Piggott (Production Manager)

Theatre includes: **Faun (Cardboard Citizens/tour); Animal, Winner's Curse (Park); Paradise Now!, Favour (& Clean Break), Red Pitch, Old Bridge (& Papatango), Overflow (Bush); Only an Octave Apart (Kindred Partners); All of Us, Barrier(s), Connections 2022 (National); The Boys are Kissing, Moreno (Theatre503); The 4th Country (Plain Heroines).**

As Deputy Production Manager, theatre includes: **The Pillowman (Empire Street Productions).**

Opera includes: **Raising Icarus (Barber Institute); The Dancing Master (Red Squirrel Opera).**

Awards include: **Olivier Award for Outstanding Achievement in Affiliate Theatre (Old Bridge).**

Jodie Underwood (Lighting Programmer)

Theatre includes: **Farm Hall (Jermyn Street); When Darkness Falls (Regional tour); Ride (West End).**

As lighting designer, theatre includes: **The Life Sporadic of Jess Wildgoose, The Man Who Thought He Knew Too Much (Pleasance); DNA (Tara); After the Act (New Diorama); Blow Down (National tour); The Boys Are Kissing (Theatre503); Dick Whittington (Met); The Three Lives of Lucie Cabroll (Rose Bruford); Elixir (Other Palace); Horse-Play (Riverside); This Is Highly Unusual (RADA); Paul Taylor Mills Summer Rep Season (Manor Pavillion/Landmark); Dido (Greenwich); The Haunting of Susan A, La Boheme (Kings Head); Us (White Bear); Dirty Corset (Soho); The Friday Freedom Fighter's (Pathway/Etcetera); Spiders Web (Regional tour).**

As lighting designer, opera includes: **La Pricess De Trebizonde (New Sussex Opera).**
As associate lighting designer, theatre includes: **Pigs Might Fly, When Darkness Falls (National tour); Ride (West End); Dig Whittington: a new dick in town (Above The Stag); Catching Comets (Pleasance/national tour).**

THE ROYAL COURT THEATRE

The Royal Court Theatre is the writers' theatre. It is a leading force in world theatre for cultivating and supporting writers – undiscovered, emerging and established.

Through the writers, the Royal Court is at the forefront of creating restless, alert, provocative theatre about now. We open our doors to the unheard voices and free thinkers that, through their writing, change our way of seeing.

Over 120,000 people visit the Royal Court in Sloane Square, London, each year and many thousands more see our work elsewhere through transfers to the West End and New York, UK and international tours, digital platforms, our residencies across London, and our site-specific work. Through all our work we strive to inspire audiences and influence future writers with radical thinking and provocative discussion.

The Royal Court's extensive development activity encompasses a diverse range of writers and artists and includes an ongoing programme of writers' attachments, readings, workshops and playwriting groups. Twenty years of the International Department's pioneering work around the world means the Royal Court has relationships with writers on every continent.

Since 1956 we have commissioned and produced hundreds of writers, from John Osborne to Jasmine Lee-Jones. Royal Court plays from every decade are now performed on stage and taught in classrooms and universities across the globe.

We strive to create an environment in which differing voices and opinions can co-exist. In current times, it is becoming increasingly difficult for writers to write what they want or need to write without fear, and we will do everything we can to rise above a narrowing of viewpoints.

It is because of this commitment to the writer and our future that we believe there is no more important theatre in the world than the Royal Court.

Supported using public funding by
ARTS COUNCIL ENGLAND

 royalcourt royalcourttheatre

ROYAL

ASSISTED PERFORMANCES

Captioned Performances

Captioned performances are accessible for people who are D/deaf, deafened & hard of hearing, as well as being suitable for people for whom English is not a first language.

Imposter 22
Thursday 12th October, 7:30pm

Blue Mist
Thursday 9th November, 3pm
Friday 10th November, 7:45pm

Mates in Chelsea
Wednesday 6th December, 7:30pm
Thursday 7th December, 2:30pm

BSL-interpreted Performances

BSL-interpreted performances, delivered by an interpreter, give a sign inteprretation of the text spoken and/or sung by artists in the onstage production.

Imposter 22
Friday 13th October, 7:30pm

Mates in Chelsea
Saturday 2nd December, 2:30pm

COURT

ASSISTED PERFORMANCES

Performances in a Relaxed Environment

Relaxed Environment performances are suitable for those who may benefit from a more relaxed environment.

During these performances:
- There is a relaxed attitude to noise in the auditorium; you are welcome to respond to the show in whatever way feels natural
- You can enter and exit the auditorium when needed
- We will help you find the best seats for your experience
- House lights may remain raised slightly
- Loud noises may be reduced

Imposter 22
All performances are relaxed.

Blue Mist
Saturday 11th November, 3pm

Mates in Chelsea
Saturday 9th December, 2:30pm

If you would like to talk to us about your access requirements, please contact our Box Office at (0)20 7565 5000 or boxoffice@royalcourttheatre.com

The Royal Court Visual Story is available on our website. Story and Sensory synposes are available on the show pages via the Whats On tab of the website shortly after Press Night.

ROYAL COURT SUPPORTERS

Our incredible community of supporters makes it possible for us to achieve our mission of nurturing and platforming writers at every stage of their careers. Our supporters are part of our essential fabric – they help to give us the freedom to take bigger and bolder risks in our work, develop and empower new voices, and create world-class theatre that challenges and disrupts the theatre ecology.

To all our supporters, thank you. You help us to write the future.

PUBLIC FUNDING

Supported using public funding by
ARTS COUNCIL ENGLAND

CHARITABLE PARTNERS

BackstageTrust

JERWOOD ARTS

CORPORATE SPONSORS

Aqua Financial Ltd
Cadogan
Edwardian Hotels, London
Sustainable Wine Solutions
Walpole

CORPORATE MEMBERS

Bloomberg Philanthopies
Cream
Sloane Stanley

TRUSTS AND FOUNDATIONS

Martin Bowley Charitable Trust
The Noël Coward Foundation
Cowley Charitable Foundation
The D'Oyly Carte Charitable Trust
The Lynne Gagliano Writer's Award
The Golden Bottle Trust
The Harold Hyam Wingate Foundation
John Lyon's Charity
Clare McIntyre's Bursary
Old Possum's Practical Trust
The Austin and Hope Pilkington Trust
Richard Radcliffe Charitable Trust
Rose Foundation
Royal Victoria Hall Foundation
John Thaw Foundation
The Victoria Wood Foundation

Royal Court Theatre
Sloane Square,
London SW1W 8AS
Tel: 020 7565 5050
info@royalcourttheatre.com
www.royalcourttheatre.com

Artistic Director
Vicky Featherstone
Interim Executive Director
Rebekah Jones*

Literary Manager
Jane Fallowfield
Senior Literary Associate
Phillippe Cato
Literary Associate
Gurnesha Bola
Open Court &
Literary Associate
Ellie Fulcher*

Associate Directors
Milli Bhatia*, Lucy Morrison, Hamish Pirie, Sam Pritchard (International).
Trainee Director
Aneesha Srinivasan

Senior Producers
Sarah Georgeson, Chris James.
Producer
Jasmyn Fisher-Ryner
International Projects Producer
Ralph Thompson
Producing Coordinator
Hannah Lyall
Assistant to the Artistic & Executive Directors
Vanessa Ng

Casting Director
Amy Ball
Casting Co-ordinator
Arthur Carrington

Open Court Associates
Mia Alizada, Jade Franks.

Living Archive
Lead Researcher & Project Co-ordinator
Sula Douglas-Folkes*
Research Assistants
Ashen Gupta*, Rosie Thackeray*.

Head of Production
Marius Rønning
Company Manager
Mica Taylor^
Head of Lighting
Deanna Towli
Lighting Technician
Max Cherry
Head of Stage
Steve Evans
Deputy Head of Stage
TJ Chappell-Meade
Stage Show Technician
Maddy Collins
Head of Sound
David McSeveney
Deputy Head of Sound
Jet Sharp
Head of Costume
Lucy Walshaw
Deputy Head of Costume
Katie Price

Finance Director
Helen Perryer
Finance Manager
Annie Moohan
Senior Finance & Payroll Officer
Will Dry
Finance & Administration Assistant
Olubukola Sonubi*

Head of People
Olivia Shaw

Director of Communications
Rachael Welsh
Press & Publicity
Bread and Butter PR
Press Officer
Ella Gold
Marketing
The 5th Wall
Managing Director
Charlotte Twining
The 5th Wall
Account Manager
Harriet Carter
Marketing Manager
Shaadi Khosravi-Rad
Marketing Assistant
Elizabeth Carpenter
Sales & Ticketing Analyst
Nicola Hobbs*

Director of Development
Katherine Osborn
Deputy Director of Development
Anuja Batra
Individual Giving Manager
Amy Millward
Trust & Foundation Manager
Sarah Bryce
Development Assistant
Nash Metaxas

Theatre Manager
Rachel Dudley
Deputy Theatre Manager
Harvey Dhadda
Duty House Manager
Jennelle Reece-Gardner
Usher/Cover Duty House Manager
Ronay Poole*
Box Office Sales Assistants
William Byam Shaw*, Ollie Harrington*, Felix Pilgrim.
Box Office & Administration Assistant
Phoebe Coop
General Maintenance Technician
David Brown
Stage Door Keepers
James Graham*, Paul Lovegrove, Holly McComish*.

Head of Operations & Sustainability
Robert Smael
Bar & Kitchen Supervisors
Ronan Cullen*, Lucy Stepan*, Milla Tikkanen*.

Manager of Samuel French Bookshop at the Royal Court Theatre
Simon Ellison
Bookshop Assistant
Terry McCormack*

Thanks to all of our Ushers and Bar & Kitchen staff.

^ The post of Company Manager is supported by Charles Holloway.

* Part-time.

ENGLISH STAGE COMPANY

President
Dame Joan Plowright CBE

Honorary Council
Alan Grieve CBE
Phyllida Lloyd CBE
Martin Paisner CBE

Council Chairman
Anthony Burton CBE
Members
Jennette Arnold OBE
Noma Dumezweni
Pamela Jikiemi
Mwenya Kawesha
James Midgley
Andrew Rodger
Anita Scott
Lord Stewart Wood
Mahdi Yahya

BAR & KITCHEN

The Royal Court's Bar & Kitchen aims to create a welcoming and inspiring environment with a style and ethos that reflects the work we put on stage.

Offering expertly crafted cocktails alongside an extensive selection of craft gins and beers, wine and soft drinks, our vibrant basement bar provides a sanctuary in the middle of Sloane Square. By day a perfect spot for meetings or quiet reflection and by night atmospheric meeting spaces for cast, crew, audiences and the general public.

All profits go directly to supporting the work of the Royal Court theatre, cultivating and supporting writers – undiscovered, emerging and established.

For more information, visit
royalcourttheatre.com/bar

HIRES & EVENTS

The Royal Court is available to hire for celebrations, rehearsals, meetings, filming, ceremonies and much more. Our two theatre spaces can be hired for conferences and showcases, and the building is a unique venue for bespoke events and receptions.

For more information, visit
royalcourttheatre.com/events

Sloane Square London, SW1W 8AS ⊖ Sloane Square ⇌ Victoria Station
🐦 royalcourt 📘 theroyalcourttheatre 📷 royalcourttheatre

SUPPORT THE COURT AND BE A PART OF OUR FUTURE.

Our Friends and Good Friends are part of the fabric of the Royal Court. They are our regulars and together, we enjoy bold and restless theatre that provokes and challenges us all. Like all friends, they help us too. The income we receive from our memberships directly supports our mission, providing writers with the space and platform to experiment and develop their writing.

Become a Friend today and inspire the next generation of theatre makers.

Become a Friend (from £40 a year)

Benefits include:

- Priority Booking
- Advanced access to £12 Monday tickets for productions in the Jerwood Theatre Downstairs
- 10% discount in our Bar & Kitchen (including Court in the Square) and Samuel French bookshop

Become a Good Friend (from £95 a year)

Our Good Friends' membership also includes a voluntary donation. This extra support goes directly towards supporting our work and future, both on and off stage.

In addition to the Friend benefits, our Good Friends also receive:

- Five complimentary playtexts for Royal Court productions
- An invitation for two to step behind the scenes of the Royal Court Theatre at a special annual event

To become a Friend or a Good Friend, or to find out more about the different ways in which you can get involved, visit our website: royalcourttheatre.com/support-us

The English Stage Company at the Royal Court Theatre is a registered charity (No. 231242)

BLUE MIST

Mohamed-Zain Dada

Acknowledgements

Thank you to Vicky Featherstone, Chris White, Sabrina Mahfouz, Ellie Fulcher and Rachel Taylor for believing in the play from the very beginning. To Jamal Mehmood for honouring me with your poem. To Milli Bhatia, for your vision, brilliance and unwavering trust. To Gurnesha Bola and Jane Fallowfield for reading every draft with a level of care that I will never forget.

To the incredible company: Tomás Palmer, Catt Padgham, Jasmyn Fisher-Ryner, Elliot Griggs, Elena Peña, Hannah Ali, Aneesha Srinivasan, Isabelle Cook, Theophilus O. Bailey and Catriona McHugh. And to everyone at the Royal Court Theatre and Nick Hern Books for all their support.

To the actors, Arian Nik, Salman Akhtar and Omar Bynon, whose generosity of spirit lit up the rehearsal room.

Special thanks to my parents, Fehmida and Ashraf Dada, my aunt, Zahida Sidik, for encouraging me to write stories as a child, Arji Manuelpillai, Benedict Lombe, Clare Callan, Zainab Hasan, Suhaiymah Manzoor-Khan, Shaykh Umar (Van Mack) and to Madani Younis for being the beacon of light in the mist.

And to Hadi Abbas, I love you, *yara*.

M-Z.D.

The poem 'White Applause in the North of England' by Jamal Mehmood was published in *The Leaf of the Neem Tree* (Hajar Press, 2021), available in paperback and ebook at hajarpress.com. It has been reproduced in this play by kind permission of Hajar Press.

'I would act as a Trojan horse that would spew forth hallucinating figures with the power to surprise, to disturb the dreams of the exploiters.'

Wilfredo Lam, 1976

Characters

JIHAD, *South Asian, twenty-five years old*
RASHID, *South Asian, twenty-four years old*
ASIF, *South Asian, twenty-four years old*

Note

The introduction of 'mist' indicates a fleeting, dreamlike state for Jihad, where the world bends to his imagination and, sometimes, doesn't.

When the mist dissipates, 'normality' returns.

This text went to press before the end of rehearsals and so may differ slightly from the play as performed.

ACT ONE

Scene One

Chunkyz Shisha Lounge. A lime-green sofa booth with a table. There are LED lights at the bottom of the sofa that periodically change from fuchsia to purple.

JIHAD enters, both RASHID and ASIF embrace him warmly.

RASHID	Bruv. He set him up with the feint and BAM.
ASIF	Solid punch, brother.
RASHID	Out cold.
	ASIF imitates the knockout punch from the night before.
	Careful, Sif, you'll injure your back, cuz.
	JIHAD and RASHID laugh. They huddle around the shisha pipe in the middle of the booth.
JIHAD	The big fight yeah?
RASHID	Yeah, J. Adam Azim, remember the name.
ASIF	Proper packed out last night.
JIHAD	Chunky screens the boxing now?
ASIF	Yeah, bruv. Pretty soon after you went uni.
JIHAD	Mad.
RASHID	Come through next time, bro.
JIHAD	Flavour's banging, what is that?
	JIHAD hands ASIF the shisha pipe.
ASIF	Super Nova mixed with Fallen Star and White Cake.

JIHAD	Bro, what?
ASIF	Chunky got Savacco now.
	ASIF *hands the pipe back to* JIHAD.
JIHAD	He's making big-boy moves.
	JIHAD *offers the pipe to* RASHID *who refuses.*
	You lot not ordering food?
RASHID	No one's ordered munch here since 2018.
ASIF	His head chef got poached by Chicken Cottage innit.
JIHAD	Cold world. Yo, do you lot know why Chunkyz closes on Thursday night?
RASHID	No idea, bro. Maybe he's sourcing new flavours.
ASIF	I do. But I can't say.
RASHID	What? You gas everything out, my g.
JIHAD	Did Chunky make you sign an NDA?
ASIF	It's his story innit.
RASHID	Oi, don't long this out, Sif.
JIHAD	I swear I won't tell a soul.
ASIF	Basically… Chunky is on *Sufi* tings innit.
JIHAD	Since when?
ASIF	Since he went Ayia Napa last year.
RASHID	HOLD ON, what? Napa? Nah, nah, you're gonna have to explain that one. 'Cause last time I checked he was posting pics of bare random buff tings on Insta.
ASIF	Yeah, I clocked that. That famous Insta model Sumz doing a lil pout with a shisha pipe.

ASIF *imitates the pout*. RASHID *laughs*.

JIHAD *laughs*.

JIHAD	Truly a confused *akhi*.
RASHID	Aren't we all in this *dunya*.
JIHAD	I'm sorry, what connects Ayia Napa and Chunky becoming a Sufi?

JIHAD *takes the shisha pipe*.

ASIF	Alright so, you know Chunky does his annual pilgrimage to Cyprus yeah? Last time he went, he was hitting all the raves, having the time of his life yeah. But there was one party. Rooftop ting. This mysterious-looking guy with long hair comes up to him and was like, 'You want to go to the best shubz in Ayia Napa?' Says to him, 'This is gonna be vibe central.'
RASHID	Anyone says 'vibe central' to me, and I'm running.
ASIF	At first, Chunky palmed them off. There are loads of people like that innit. Random crackheads, bare people hustling. But this guy was insisting, kept saying he'd find the best music, weed and girls at this party.
RASHID	The magic trio.
ASIF	Chunky said he had this look in his eye, a look that told him it was legit. He weren't your bog-standard Cypriot hustler.
JIHAD	Did he go?
ASIF	Chunky convinced his boys. They left the rave they were at and this mystery dude with a silver helmet told them to follow him on his moped.
JIHAD	Lemme get this straight. Chunky is trusting random Daft Punk-looking Cypriot breh?

And they end up following this guy on his moped? Sounds dubious at best, Sif.

ASIF   Apparently. 'Cause they were following him for ages until this guy needed to stop to use the loo.
            But they ended up at a *maqam*.

RASHID   What's that?

ASIF   Like where a saint is buried innit.

RASHID   Did they follow moped guy inside?

ASIF   Yeah, Chunky was curious.

JIHAD   Fair enough.

ASIF   Anyways, they go inside, and Chunky said most his boys left after that. They thought that this moped guy was taking them on some wild gooseberry chase.

JIHAD   Wild goose chase, Sif.

ASIF   After that moped guy said, 'This ain't where the party is.'

JIHAD   Did Chunky go with him?

ASIF   He said he was just transfixed by the guy so he decided to follow and go, yeah.

RASHID   Kashmiri Braveheart.

JIHAD   My guy has no brains.

ASIF   Now they are back on the road. They'd been driving for about two, three hours yeah, further and further away from Napa.

JIHAD   Wasn't Chunky scared? Or suspicious?

ASIF   I don't know. But at this point, it was like proper late.
            Imagine though yeah, a full moon, felt like a big night. And finally they got to this

random village. Chunky said, he's never seen so many cats.

RASHID	Cats? Like people?
ASIF	Nah, as in pussycats innit.
RASHID	I gotta find this place.
JIHAD	(*To* RASHID.) Bruv, he means actual cats.
RASHID	I still wanna go, not gonna lie.
ASIF	So Chunky got out his car, no sign of any shubz. Or weed. Still, he follows moped dude into the centre. And then.
JIHAD	And then?
ASIF	They got to there, and Chunky says it was like some *Assassin's Creed* shit.
JIHAD	What do you mean?
ASIF	Like it was like Ottoman times innit. Old-looking houses and then this huge castle-like mosque in the middle…
	…It was like the Muslim Hogwarts.
RASHID	Abu Hamza and the Prisoner of Azka-Belmarsh.
	They laugh.
ASIF	All Chunky could hear is rhythmic chanting. So moped guy and him went into this castle and when he got to the main hall… hundreds of people were doing *Dhikr*.
JIHAD	Sounds like a cult.
RASHID	Jeez.
ASIF	This is where it gets a bit… magical innit. I shouldn't.
JIHAD	What? What happened next?

RASHID   Sif? Carry on, bruv.

ASIF   Gotta to make sure he's not listening to me
                telling this innit. He didn't really wanna
                share it.

JIHAD   Who are we gonna tell, Sif?

RASHID   Bro, *Allah Ki Kasam,* I won't tell anyone.

ASIF   Say swear.

RASHID   I just did, you *lulli*.

ASIF   Oh shit yeah. J?

JIHAD   I promise, Siffy.

ASIF   Alright cool. Basically. When Chunky sat
                down to join in… they were reciting Allah's
                name. But like breathing in and out too.
                Chunky was a bit baffled at first, but his heart
                told him to join in, so he did.

                And it was pitch black yeah. Except for this
                one green light at the back. Chunky said, he
                couldn't help but focus on it. Like it was
                a guiding light.

                Like looking at infinity.

                But then…

                ASIF *leans in and whispers.*

                As Chunky was in the zone. He looks out the
                corner of his eye, away from the green light,
                and he saw someone was…

JIHAD   Was what, Sif?

ASIF   – afloat.

RASHID   Eh?

JIHAD   You what?
                Float? What like hot-air balloons?

ASIF   Floating toward the ceiling, bro.

JIHAD   Nah nah, this is bollocks, Sif.

                 RASHID *stands in fake outrage*.

RASHID   That's not possible, g. Like physically innit.

                 JIHAD *takes the shisha pipe back from* ASIF.

JIHAD   Thank you, esteemed astrophysicist Dr Rashid.

                 RASHID *sits back down*.

ASIF   *Kasmeh*.

                 I know it's wild, but – I-I believe it. I can tell
                 when Chunky chats shit.

JIHAD   Did they split the moon too? With their
                 magical Sufi powers?

RASHID   Sounds like *bi'dah*.

ASIF   *Dhikr* ain't *bi'dah*, Rash, don't be a wobbler.
                 You lot aren't understanding the deeper
                 meaning.

JIHAD   Which is what, Sif?

ASIF   You see love, yeah? If it's sincere, and it's in
                 your heart, it can spill over yeah. And if that
                 feeling is strong, it rises and rises like a
                 bubble until –

RASHID   – POP.

JIHAD   You sound like Jay Shetty, Sif.

                 RASHID *laughs*.

ASIF   You lot are *haraamis*.

RASHID   Nah for real, Sif, that's deep, bro.

JIHAD   Hold up, Sif, so what happened to moped guy?

ASIF   Chunky said, after he left, he looked
                 everywhere for moped guy, but couldn't
                 find him.

JIHAD	Daft Punk lost in Northern Cyprus. Even though this is complete rubbish, Sif, it could be a sick premise for a YA novel.
RASHID	You should do that, J. Make millions innit.
ASIF	You'd be the Asian J. K. Rowling.
	P. K. Rowling.
	RASHID *laughs*. JIHAD *smiles*.
JIHAD	Nah but seriously, that's a mad story, Sif.
RASHID	Yo I forgot he closes on Thursday nights, always messes up my date-night plans with Hanifa.
ASIF	Yeah apparently, loads of Sufi dons turn up.
RASHID	Break-dancing and shit.
ASIF	Rash, bro?
	JIHAD *laughs*. ASIF *looks irritated*.
RASHID	Sorry, *yara*. Tell me one thing yeah, why'd Chunky tell you?
ASIF	I'm a trustworthy guy innit. I thought J would have the inside scoop. Big-time journalist and that.
RASHID	Oyy, how's that going, J?
ASIF	You been tryna get into this for time. They racist or something?
JIHAD	D-d-on't really wanna chat about it, boys.
RASHID	What you talking about, bro.
JIHAD	It's not even worth getting into.
ASIF	Nah, J. C'mon, bruv?
JIHAD	Nah, Sif, that dream's dead, alright. It's done.
RASHID	My bro. J. You know you're the smartest person I know.

ASIF	Second smartest for me, on current league standing innit.
	I have an uncle who worked for Pa-fizer. Scientist.
JIHAD	It's just Pfizer, Sif, silent 'P'.
RASHID	J. If anyone has the smarts to do this. To break through. It's you. I truly believe that.
	Hand on heart, *yara*.
JIHAD	You boys don't get it. I literally can't keep doing this. All that work and for what? I got nothing to show for it and I've made no fucking progress.
	Like at a certain point it's just embarrassing.
	RASHID *looks at* ASIF.
ASIF	J. If you're not gonna do it for you, do it for us.
JIHAD	What you talking about?
ASIF	I mean, it's sick we're all back together chilling at Chunkyz but we always knew you were gonna go and do bits.
RASHID	Trust me, Sif.
ASIF	You could email ITV innit. That guy er, what's his name, Faisal Islam?
	Pause.
RASHID	There's gotta be something, J?
JIHAD	There is, there is a competition. I wasn't even gonna apply but it's a mad opportunity.
RASHID	There we go, bruv. There we go.
JIHAD	I dunno if I can take another rejection.
ASIF	What's the competition?

JIHAD	It's this new media outlet called Ajami. Like they'd be exactly the kind of place I'd love to work for. They make these incredible documentaries. And this thing is for like aspiring journalists, you send them an idea and if you win, they help you produce it –
ASIF	– Let's come up with something RIGHT now.
JIHAD	I don't have the energy, Sif.
RASHID	Nah, J, we're gonna do this. What you got, Sif?
JIHAD	Boys, I really dunno.
ASIF	Something on why Changez' uncle has no *tidd*.
JIHAD	Sorry, can you please explain that?
RASHID	What?
ASIF	I have a theory yeah, you see people who get their teeth and hair done in Turkey. Certain uncles are flying out to get liposuction on their *tidd*.
RASHID	Sif, where are are you hearing this?
JIHAD	How would that even work?
ASIF	You know girls get them BBLs. Uncles also get BBL. But it's Brazilian Belly Loss. Then they take the *boti* from the mans, and add it to the womans. Nothing is wasted.
JIHAD	You're talking about belly fat like it's left-over haleem.
RASHID	Let me get this straight yeah, there is some girl who's done her BBL and she doesn't know she's got some random uncle's belly fat on her *bunda*.
ASIF	I don't know it for a fact, but that's what Jihad could investigate.
RASHID	PFC-powered *gand*.

JIHAD	Might be a bit niche, Sif.
ASIF	I'd watch it.
RASHID	Bruv, what about a thing on Pakistani boxers? There's bare of them now.
JIHAD	Banging idea, but hard to get in touch with them.
ASIF	My *khala's* cousin's father-in-law might know Shabaz Masoud you know.
JIHAD	As much as I appreciate this brainstorming sesh, boys –
ASIF	– Wait I have another idea.
RASHID	Here we go.
ASIF	What about… something on Chunkyz?
	Pause.
RASHID	What about him though?
JIHAD	Nah, that's actually… really good, Sif.
ASIF	Is it?
JIHAD	Yeah, Sif. It's banging. It's newsworthy. Interesting and it's got a political edge too.
RASHID	Serious?
JIHAD	Yeah yeah. Certain politicians here want to ban them like in Toronto.
RASHID	Nah, they seriously banned them out there?
JIHAD	Yeah, Rash.
ASIF	I didn't know the Canadian lot moved like that.
RASHID	Probably 'cause they're part-French innit.
JIHAD	That's why this could be so good. We get to have a voice before these politicians say shit for us.

RASHID	And people will watch that kinda thing?
JIHAD	It's an audio documentary, Rash.
RASHID	Audio as in radio?
JIHAD	Yeah, like a podcast.
RASHID	I don't really get it, J. People are gonna sit around and listen to some shit about Chunkyz?
ASIF	I reckon they will. He's got mad stories.
JIHAD	Not just Chunkyz. The wider social picture. Why us lot value it. What it means to us. That's the one. That's it! Sif, you're a genius.
ASIF	My mum says that too.
RASHID	Alright if you're gonna go with this, J. I got an idea for the name...
JIHAD	Hit me.
RASHID	*PIPE DREAMS*.
ASIF	Yo that's SICK.
JIHAD	I love it, Rash. I love it.
RASHID	Obviously, we're always here at Chunkyz cooking up plans innit.
ASIF	You might have to buy copyright from a plumbing company in Luton though.
JIHAD	You lot got me on a boost now.
RASHID	Do me a favour, J, go and win this competition. Do it for us innit.
ASIF	And I want a ten-per-cent cut.
RASHID	Zardari over here already negotiating.
JIHAD	You can have anything you want if I pull this off.

Scene Two

Jihad's bedroom.

JIHAD   Record a two-minute summary, okay.

JIHAD *takes a deep breath. Starts recording.*

Ahem. *Pipe Dreams*, documenting shisha culture in the UK.

Hi. I am Jihad Hussain. Ahem. I'm a reporter with –

Alright.

JIHAD *imitates Shah Rukh Khan.*

I am Jihad. And I am not a terrorist.

He laughs to himself.

Okay. Okay. Serious. Serious.

I'm Jihad Hussain. A freelance journalist and documentary-maker, here to tell you all about the subcultures that are rarely covered –

– I sound like a fucking *Vice* reporter. That is not it.

JIHAD *attempts to sing like Chunkz.*

Hey yea-aaaah, it's your boy, JH the journalist.

Follow me @JihadTheJournalist, remember to like and subscribe.

Nah. Cringe.

A slither of mist. ASIF *enters as* FIONA – *a journalist and producer for Ajami Media.*

ASIF/FIONA   The winning idea will receive a cash prize and will be produced by Ajami Media. An award-winning platform where context matters. Grounded in truth, a place where facts really mean something.

Ajami. The home of serious journalism.

This is Fiona Matthews, BAFTA-winning journalist reporting from a disputed border.

ASIF/FIONA *exits*.

What sounds like the start of a news report morphs into a fast-paced beat.

JIHAD   I am Jihad Hussain for Ajami Media.
An insurgent news start-up. Questioning the status quo.
Unafraid to ask the difficult questions.

Facing up to corruption.
Lies.
Deceit.

Making original documentaries. I don't give a shit what you say, I'm here to stay. In a world where fake news dominates, where truth is shut down and silenced.

Bombs dropping.

In war zones.
Grilling the dictators,
and standing up to arms dealers,
interrogating the prime minister,
to corrupt local councillors,

He grabs an umbrella. Heavy winds.

the climate crisis and facing up to the energy companies.

Helicopters circling.

At Davos, confronting the super-rich.
Award-winning. Critically acclaimed.
The face of serious journalism.

The beat drops and JIHAD *dances as if he's in a rave.*

Serious, serious journalism.
Serious, serious journalism.
Serious, serious journalism.
Serious, serious journalism.

JIHAD *continues to dance until it gets awkward and the mist disappears.*

Recording.

Alright, let's do this!

Shisha lounges, from Pasha in Bradford to Silk in Park Royal, are a place to call home for lots of Muslim youth. An alternative to pubs, where you can grab a pipe, socialise, laugh, dream and scheme. Every lounge is different. From the old-school cafés where backgammon is played by Arab uncles to the bougie spots where you have to take a mortgage out to buy VOSS water. Options are endless.

But there is no place as special as Chunkyz Shisha Lounge – where legendary moments are enshrined in local folklore. Only at a place like Chunkyz can you launch a new shisha flavour and fashion line called the Magna *Kurta.*

JIHAD *pauses for effect.*

Pipe Dreams: the story behind one of Britain's craziest shisha lounges, and what it means to a community.

JIHAD *does a quick* dua.

Bismillah!

Incoming email.

AJAMI MEDIA Dear Ji-Had,

I hope this email finds you well. Thanks for your patience as we waded through over five

hundred submissions for the Ajami Media
Future Documentary-Maker Award. The
judges were impressed with your proposal,
Pipe Dreams. They particularly loved the
authenticity of your voice.

It was an incredibly tough decision, with so
many high-quality entrants, including
yourself. But we are pleased to say that you
are the official winner of the Ajami Media
Future Documentary-Maker Award!

Our team at Ajami Media will be in touch
about next steps, but for now, wishing you a
hearty congratulations from everyone here.

Best regards,

Matty. Kiss.

Scene Three

RASHID *and* JIHAD *are at Chunkyz Shisha Lounge.* JIHAD *is*
smoking shisha. RASHID *is recording.*

RASHID   I don't even like shisha, bruv. Impacts my
                    gains. But it's a social ting innit. I'm a retired
                    raver. Don't drink. What else we gonna do?
                    Some people have a pint. Some people have a
                    pipe. We all need a release. I don't care what
                    anyone says yeah, everyone needs a place to
                    be themselves innit.
                    Where else would we go?

                    JIHAD *stops recording.*

                    Bruv, who in their right mind wants to hear us
                    chat shit all day?

JIHAD   Bro. There is a beauty in your words, trust me.

RASHID	Sign me up for a breakfast radio slot then innit, I'll quit Heathrow.
JIHAD	Where's Sif?
RASHID	Dunno. Said he had a 'commitment'.
JIHAD	What kind of commitment?
RASHID	Them ones innit.
JIHAD	You know what, if it's a girl he's seeing. I'm happy for Sif.
RASHID	Hold up, J. I just clocked what we're missing…
JIHAD	What?
	RASHID *stands up*.
RASHID	Sparklers innit!
	will.i.am & Cody Wise's 'It's My Birthday' starts playing. RASHID *brings out a shisha pipe and a tart with a candle and sparklers. He hands it to* JIHAD, *who puts his head in his hands.*
	RASHID *laughs*.
	Man like Asad Ahmad, BBC News.
JIHAD	It's minor, bro.
RASHID	Nah it's not MINOR, bruv. This is BIG news, J. Bare people must have applied.
	RASHID *sits back down*.
	Am I gonna be on radio?
JIHAD	If they decide to produce it.
RASHID	I thought you won the competition?
JIHAD	Yeah. Yeah I did. But erm.
RASHID	But what?
JIHAD	They might not like what I come up with.

RASHID   You won for a reason, J. Own it, my bro. Yo,
                you gotta interview Chunky.

                RASHID *imitates Chunky – a hybrid of
                Bradford and Mirpur.*

                'I've dreamed of starting this lounge since
                I was a child in Kashmir. I looked at the
                clouds rising above Azad Kashmir and
                thought, Shisha… Huqqa… That is when
                I knew my destiny.'

JIHAD   One hundred per cent. The man is a living
                legend.

RASHID   For real. You know he told me back in the
                day, you could get people into the UK bare
                easy. In the seventies and eighties. He got his
                cousin from Kashmir in his boot, bruv.

JIHAD   He drove to Kashmir?

RASHID   Nah he picked him up from Calais in France
                innit.

JIHAD   They didn't do any checks?

RASHID   Listen to this yeah, when Chunky got to
                Dover and the border lot checked the boot, his
                cousin ran out and hid in a bush. But these
                were the days with no phones innit, so
                Chunky ended up staying in a hotel one night
                until he found his cousin in some next café
                with a cuppa and a full English breakfast,
                obviously no sausage.

JIHAD   My man was integrating on day one.

RASHID   Trust. How comes I didn't see you at *Jummah*
                today, J?

JIHAD   I-I erm, prayed somewhere else innit.

RASHID   Bruv, you missed a madness.

JIHAD   What happened?

RASHID   These lot kill me. So some youngish brother, the Qur'an *hafiz*, think his name is Farooq, he came through and made an announcement saying that they'll be screening the boxing this Saturday. To get the youth in yeah?

             RASHID *gets up and imitates the man in the mosque.*

             Soon as he gets up though, Uncle Haram gets up too.

             With that Dr Zakir Naik swag. Chapter, verse and index finger prepped.

             'WHAT ABOUT THE RING GIRLS? DO WE WANT OUR YOUTH EXPOSED TO RING GIRLS?'

             Farooq is frozen, J.

             He mumbles something about ring girls being blurred out. Saying this is something they should discuss after *Jummah*. Uncle Haram keeps shouting out.

             'Ring girls and all they wear is LIN-GER-RIE.'

             Bruv, I had to suppress my laughter but I burst out when he said that.

             Next thing you know, a couple uncles try calm him down. AND THEN, the Imam comes through calling this uncle an 'idiot'.

             FULL-BLOWN BEEF TING.

             At this point, couple brothers are tryna stop Uncle Haram, trying to get him to sit down but he keeps going. 'Naked body. Men doing full waxing. Women in panty. THAT is the promotion of PAN-AG-RA-PHY.'

JIHAD   Uncle's got bars.

RASHID   The Imam looks like he's gonna explode in
               anger, J. And he just uses the mic to start
               shouting:

               'THIS IS NOT THE FIRST TIME, NOT THE
               SECOND BUT THE THIRD TIME YOU
               HAVE INTERRUPTED DURING *JUMMAH*
               PRAYER.'

               I'm like, 'Gwan, Shaykh Ahmed, SLEW HIM.'

               Uncle Haram is fuming, but at this point,
               other brothers are taking him to the back. All
               you can hear him shouting is:

               'HARAAAAM. IT IS HARAAAAM.' It's
               like if *EastEnders* had only Muslim uncles as
               characters.

               JIHAD *laughs*.

JIHAD   These uncles need to get a grip.

RASHID   Oi, you should pitch that idea to your work
               lot, J. Like instead of *Twenty-Four Hours in
               A&E*, *Twenty-Four Hours at* Jummah.

JIHAD   Erm, I dunno if it works like that, bro –

RASHID   – Actually, you know what, dead that idea.
               How about this. Picture it: eight aunties
               prepare to go Pakistan. They have ONE
               suitcase each and bare items to take. They have
               eight minutes to fit as much as they can and
               they can only take a certain amount of KG.

               The AUNTY who gets the MOST amount of
               stuff within the weight allowance gets a free
               trip to Pakistan.

JIHAD   I might actually have to steal that, Rash.
               How's Hanifa doing by the way?

RASHID   Hani's good, bro, she told me to congratulate
               you innit.

JIHAD	Give her my love, Rash. When we congratulating you two then?
RASHID	Marriage?
JIHAD	Yeah.
RASHID	She wants to.
JIHAD	You don't?
RASHID	Settle down with what, J? What is man gonna give as a *Mehr*? My uncle's two pet cows from Jhelum?
JIHAD	What about that business idea?
	Pause.
RASHID	You wanna hear what I got?
JIHAD	Go on.
RASHID	Imagine this yeah: Aunties. Only. Gym. No pervs. No stress about mans looking at you. A place to just be yourself.
JIHAD	It's actually a banging idea, Rash. Why Aunties-only though? You gonna ban leggings?
RASHID	The strict rule would be you can only work out in a bright-orange shalwar kameez and Arch Fit Skechers.
	They both laugh.
	Nah but seriously, all aunties do is give in this *dunya*, I just wanna give a little bit back.
JIHAD	I mean it's a sick idea.
RASHID	You wanna hear the name?
JIHAD	Go on… you clearly got a knack for it.
RASHID	HENCHISM.
JIHAD	Henchism?
RASHID	HENCHISM.

JIHAD	As in Hench and?
RASHID	Ism at the end, you got it. It's not just a name, J…
RASHID/JIHAD	It's a lifestyle.
RASHID	YO! How did you know?
JIHAD	Lucky guess. I'm proud of you, Rash.
RASHID	Only way to get out this rat race, my bro.
JIHAD	How you gonna fund it?
RASHID	Don't say anything yeah, but I'm thinking of chatting to Haz.
JIHAD	Haz? Bro, doesn't he sell steroids under the counter at his own gym? You think that's a good idea? Especially 'cause of your record.
RASHID	Yo, keep your voice down, J.
JIHAD	Shit, sorry.
RASHID	You know how hard it is for me to get a bank loan?
JIHAD	I don't get it. You made one mistake when you were fourteen, so what? But a partnership with Haz? I don't know.
RASHID	I've not asked him yet innit, and dunno if I will, but who am I to judge people, J?
JIHAD	I hear you, be careful though.
RASHID	Course, J. Or I could ask you to put money in when you blow up, *Inshallah*.
JIHAD	Bro, I'll be the first one to invest.
RASHID	Love, J.

Scene Four

Jihad's bedroom/office.

JIHAD	(*Audio*.) Where do you come from?
CHUNKY	(*Audio*.) Azad Kashmir.
JIHAD	(*Audio*.) Why did you open Chunkyz Shisha Lounge?
CHUNKY	(*Audio*.) A long time ago, brother, I saw a movie. I think it was call *Selena*.
JIHAD	(*Audio*.) *Selena*?
CHUNKY	(*Audio*.) Ya. Ya. It had Jennifer Lopez.
JIHAD	(*Audio*.) Jennifer Lopez? The singer yeah?
CHUNKY	(*Audio*.) I'm still, I'm still Jenny from block, yes.
JIHAD	(*Audio*.) What's that gotta do with Chunkyz?
CHUNKY	(*Audio*.) I'm telling you *enneh*. In the movie, she plays a singer who go from Mexico to America. And when she come back to Mexico after being singer, Mexicans say she has to prove she is still Mexican. Jenny father also say they have to show they are more American too. More Mexican than Mexicans. More American than Americans. So I want to make a place that remind me of back home *enneh*.
JIHAD	(*Audio*.) You wanted to recreate Azad Kashmir... At Chunkyz?
CHUNKY	(*Audio*.) *Haan Ji!* I even call it Azad Lounge first.
JIHAD	(*Audio*.) Freedom Lounge?

CHUNKY   (*Audio*.) Ya, but my accountant, Mushy, told
                me to name it after me.

                JIHAD *smiles. Starts recording.*

JIHAD   Chunky articulated a sentiment felt by most
                young people of colour and the generations
                who came before them. The idea that
                migrants channel their longing into the spaces
                we end up calling home. And through that
                process, end up creating somewhere new.

                I call these spaces the borderlands. A place for
                people who have to spend their life on the
                margins. The loopholes in the matrix. In light
                of the threats to shisha lounges being
                suggested by politicians in the UK, lounges
                like Chunkyz are more important then ever.

                ASIF/FIONA *enters.*

ASIF/FIONA   Hello again, Ji-Had.

JIHAD   Hi Fiona, you can call me J.

ASIF/FIONA   No, Ji-Had, I really value the importance of
                names.

JIHAD   I mean even my friends call me –

ASIF/FIONA   – I love what you've sent so far. Particularly,
                Chunky?

JIHAD   Yes.

ASIF/FIONA   Great storytelling.
                I think you have so much potential, Ji-Had.

JIHAD   Really?

ASIF/FIONA   Truly. But, but, and I don't mean to go all
                'But-istan' on you, BUT…

                At Ajami, we like to push the boundaries…
                really shake things up.

JIHAD   I mean.

ASIF/FIONA   I believe you can go a lot further with the
                 narrative.

JIHAD   In what way?

ASIF/FIONA   Don't be afraid to show the good, the bad and
                 ugly –

JIHAD   – I was thinking like, Chunkyz and other
                 spaces being like portals into people's lives.
                 Like, Chunky's journey from Kashmir, and
                 like, other shisha owners of other backgrounds
                 talking about their journeys to Britain.
                 Sort of like how these people create a new life
                 and a kind of new space for people who come
                 after them.

                 Pause.

                 What do you think?

ASIF/FIONA   I completely agree. My instinct tells me –

                 Pause.

                 – that this documentary is less about lounges
                 and more about 'masculinity'. South Asian
                 Muslim masculinity.

JIHAD   Sure yeah. Okay cool so I should –

ASIF/FIONA   – Tap into that. That vulnerable core.

JIHAD   Thank you, Fiona.

ASIF/FIONA   I've got high expectations, Ji-Had, but I'm
                 convinced you're going to deliver.

                 A slither of mist. ASIF/FIONA *brings out
                 a pack of cards as if they're playing UNO.*

                 ASIF/FIONA *slams the first card down.*

                 Grooming.

JIHAD	Male grooming. Afghan barbers.
ASIF/FIONA	Honour killings.
JIHAD	White supremacy.
ASIF/FIONA	Cultural insularity.

JIHAD *collects the cards, he's on the back foot.*

JIHAD	Eton.
ASIF/FIONA	Casual misogyny.
JIHAD	Grunwick Strike.
ASIF/FIONA	Victimhood narrative.
JIHAD	Drone bombing. UNO!

ASIF/FIONA *panics.*

ASIF/FIONA	Erm. BAME voices.
JIHAD	Tokenism.

RASHID *enters as* MIKE, *CEO of Ajami Media, and sweeps the cards to the floor.*

ASIF/FIONA	This is Mike.
JIHAD	The CEO of Ajami Media?
RASHID/MIKE	We are shaking up the media landscape.
JIHAD	You like the idea?
RASHID/MIKE	I do.
ASIF/FIONA	*Pipe Dreams.*
RASHID/MIKE	Nightmares.
ASIF/FIONA	Audiences don't want to hear a university lecture.
RASHID/MIKE	Tension.

ASIF/FIONA   They want an arc.

RASHID/MIKE   Blood.

JIHAD   What?

RASHID/MIKE   It sells.

ASIF/FIONA   They want balance.

JIHAD   Really?

RASHID/MIKE   That's why we both wear New Balance.

RASHID *and* ASIF *exit.*

JIHAD *leaves briefly and transforms into Mary Poppins. He emerges out of the smoke like a contestant in* Stars in Their Eyes. *'A Spoonful of Sugar' from* Mary Poppins, *sung by Julie Andrews, plays in the background. We hear the first verse and then –*

JIHAD   (*Singing.*)
A spoonful of Muslim helps the news go down.
The news go down.
The news go down.
Just a spoonful of Muslim helps the news
    go down.
In the most alarming way.

A journalist feathering his nest,
Must always pander to the West,
Gathering their bits of lies that stick,
Though dogged in their pursuit,
A merry whistle they will toot,
He knows a Muslim will move the job along!

ASIF *re-enters with a Daft Punk helmet on. The sound of a qawwal singing, cascading, echoes in the background.*

Y-y-y-ou?

ASIF/QALANDAR
            What is good?

JIHAD   Whatever is good for me.

ASIF/QALANDAR
            What is bad?

JIHAD   Whatever is bad for me.

ASIF/QALANDAR
            What is evil?

JIHAD   I have no idea.

ASIF/QALANDAR
            Where are you going?

JIHAD   I do not know.

ASIF/QALANDAR
            Sink or float?

ACT TWO

Scene One

Jihad's bedroom/office. JIHAD *writes furiously.*

Recording.

JIHAD	Let's call this for what it is. Local councils might say shisha lounges lack planning permission or operate illegally, but we know that the spaces that happen to be dominated by Muslim communities get a completely disproportionate level of attention.
	It's not so much that shisha is bad for your lungs, but that the people smoking it are bad for society.
	A phone call. ASIF/FIONA *enters.*
ASIF/FIONA	Ji-Had?
JIHAD	H-Hi-Hello, Fiona. Did you manage to hear the clips I sent through?
ASIF/FIONA	I did. Fascinating… analysis.
	Pause.
	Do you remember my documentary on honour killings, Ji-Had?
JIHAD	It was… horrific. I actually had some questions about the sort of wider narrative you showed –
ASIF/FIONA	– Brutal, right? A family torn apart by a warped sense of cultural norms.
JIHAD	Right, yes exactly.

ASIF/FIONA   I couldn't make that in today's age.

JIHAD   Why not.

ASIF/FIONA   Ji-Had, I recognise that the conversation has moved forward. It wouldn't be right for me to front that up, given I'm –

– someone of a *different* identity. That's why it's necessary to have new voices coming through.

JIHAD   I'm grateful for the opportunity, Fiona.

ASIF/FIONA   Good. Because I have some thoughts.

JIHAD   Yeah, p-please tell me.

ASIF/FIONA   I love that you've interviewed those friends, As-eef and Ra-sheed.

JIHAD   Great.

ASIF/FIONA   But who are they? What are they fighting to achieve as Asian Muslim men in British society? What are their struggles, Ji-Had?

JIHAD   Erm.

ASIF/FIONA   Anything you can share?
Anything at all?

JIHAD   I'm trying to think if there is –
Asif works at a car-rental company?

ASIF/FIONA   Okay?

JIHAD   And Rash works for Heathrow.

ASIF/FIONA   Right.

JIHAD   Yeah but erm, I'm not sure what else.

Pause.

ASIF/FIONA   If there isn't anything else. It might be that this idea doesn't quite fit that Ajami mould. Which is totally okay, Ji-Had. It would be

	a great developmental experience for you either way –
JIHAD	– No I mean there are other things.
ASIF/FIONA	There are?
JIHAD	Like erm, Rash is really making an amazing life for himself, with this gym concept he's got. Even though he's had a bit of trouble in the past.
ASIF/FIONA	Trouble in the past?
JIHAD	Oh yeah erm.
ASIF/FIONA	What kind of trouble?
JIHAD	He was standing up for his aunt and uncle against this kid and –
ASIF/FIONA	– A fight?
JIHAD	– Yeah, it was pretty bad but –
ASIF/FIONA	– A fight with a kid? Was he arrested?
JIHAD	I mean Rash was a kid himself but I dunno if that's –
ASIF/FIONA	– A youth offender?
JIHAD	Yeah but –
ASIF/FIONA	– There we are.
JIHAD	What do you mean?
ASIF/FIONA	That's context, Ji-Had.
	Pause.
JIHAD	This is, this isn't really something I'd want to share though.
	Pause.
ASIF/FIONA	We can't shy away from the truth, Ji-Had.
	A moment.

JIHAD   It just feels really far from what I pitched and
                   erm –

ASIF/FIONA   – Ji-Had. If we aren't brave enough to speak
                   to these issues, the vacuum is filled by
                   journalists with bad intentions.

JIHAD   I understand that but –

ASIF/FIONA   – And that's why you won the Ajami
                   competition.
                   Because you were exactly what we were
                   looking for.

JIHAD   I was?

ASIF/FIONA   We had big plans for you, Ji-Had.

JIHAD   I hope I can show you why I won… this
                   competition, Fiona.

ASIF/FIONA   Remember, a good journalist doesn't always
                   play friendly, in fact they mostly don't.

                   *Blue mist surrounds him. A distorted version
                   of Dave & Central Cee's 'Trojan Horse' starts
                   playing.*

                   Negative affirmations echo and reverberate.

MUSLIM ENTREPRENEUR
                   If you ain't got at least two Lambos, don't
                   chat to me, bruv.

ASIF   Big-time journalist yeah?

MUSLIM ENTREPRENEUR
                   How to start a Halal e-commerce store.
                   Subscribe now to learn how to engage in
                   Halal drop-shipping.

WAKEY WINES IMPRESSION
                   Bingo Bingo, Gala Bingo.

JIHAD   Change the system from the inside.

MUSLIM ENTREPRENEUR
          Imagine after all those books, and you still
          can't get your money up.

JIHAD'S FATHER
          Beta, there is no future in this.

WAKEY WINES IMPRESSION
          Abdul, come closer.

JIHAD   Get your foot in the door first.

ASIF   My guy is always leaking shit.

JIHAD   Make this, then make whatever you like.

MR PHILLIPS, JIHAD'S SCHOOLTEACHER
          Not with that name.

          Not with that name.

ASIF/FIONA   We had big plans for you, Ji-Had.

Scene Two

Chunkyz Shisha Lounge. RASHID *is sat on a sofa.* JIHAD
enters.

RASHID   Salaam, my bro.

JIHAD   Yes, Rash.

RASHID   Yo, lemme get –

          ASIF *enters in a huff and puff wearing a suit.*

          Yo, Sif, you just get back from work?
          What's going on? Why d'you look depressed,
          bruv.

JIHAD   Yeah, where you been?

ASIF   Fuck these dating apps, bruv.

RASHID *and* JIHAD *laugh.*

RASHID   What happened, Sif?

ASIF *grabs the shisha pipe.*

ASIF   Muslims, bruv.

ASIF *blows out smoke.*

RASHID   Slow down, my g.

JIHAD   Give it a chance, Sif. You can't knock these apps so early.

ASIF   Bruv, I have. This isn't the first time. Remember the Romford *Rundi*?

JIHAD   Nah?

RASHID   The girl who two-timed him innit.

ASIF   Girls are asking all sorts nowadays.

RASHID   Like what?

ASIF   Like, er, if I have my own yard? I mean, who does these days? Who?

RASHID   I mean, you got the Aslam brothers, the ones who own that cash and carry, the Khan brothers. Jihad's dad.

ASIF   I meant, which *young person* innit.

RASHID   Oh, then you got Haz and I'm pretty sure Chunky's got a few properties.

JIHAD   Bare juiced-up *akhis* funding Haz's property portfolio.

RASHID   Keep your voice down, J.

ASIF   I heard he puts them in mango lassi and downs it.

RASHID   Bruv, where do you hear these rumours?

JIHAD   Rash, to be fair, this is the same guy that thinks Chunky can fly like Superman.

RASHID	Pak Man. Aka Chunky Kent.

They laugh.

JIHAD	I would not put it past Chunky to have one two yards in Cannes.
ASIF	Is Chunky still young? Mans got grey hairs on his ponytail.
JIHAD	That man has drunk the shisha fountain of youth.
RASHID	How do you find a wifey with your thumb anyway?
ASIF	You heard about Uncle Shauqat from Al-Furqan?
JIHAD	Hold up, boys, I'm recording this for the documentary thing yeah?

He starts recording.

ASIF	Go for it, J.
RASHID	Nah, what's going on with him?
JIHAD	This is the uncle that does the *adhaan* right, at the Al-Furqan mosque?
ASIF	Yeah, he's married already, but went on Single Muslim to find a second wife.
JIHAD	That's messed up, man.
RASHID	Did the first know?
ASIF	Nah… She didn't. To be fair, J, he does have three daughters, that's terrible luck.

RASHID *slaps* ASIF *playfully once, and a second time a bit harder.*

Ow, bruv.

RASHID	Second slap was from Hani. She'd have slapped you too.

ASIF	I'm saying it's terrible luck for certain backward uncles innit.
RASHID	Half these man just wants to get with a woman half their age.
JIHAD	Trust me. Where do you think attitude comes from, Rash?
	Pause.
RASHID	Probably too much monosodium in their diet innit.
ASIF	What?
RASHID	I read something about Chinese salt making older mans horny. Siffy, what you looking for, my bro?
	JIHAD *takes the shisha pipe.*
ASIF	Brothers, I'm looking for wifey. Someone on deen. With a good heart. Beautiful smile.
	ASIF *pauses.*
	Most importantly, someone who can help me and Mum at home innit.
JIHAD	A roti expert.
	RASHID *laughs.*
RASHID	'Preferably two to five years' experience in making regular *rotiya*.'
ASIF	I actually make the rotis for Afz. Can you lot make *rotiya*?
JIHAD	I – erm.
RASHID	Ask your mum then innit, Sif? *Rishta* flex?
ASIF	Nah, Mum's just gonna show me girls from back home. And do you think Suella de Vil is gonna let a new foreign wifey get a shiny red passport?

JIHAD	I think it's blue now.
RASHID	Haz done that. Got married in Morocco and brought her here innit.
ASIF	Is it?
RASHID	Yep, new Moroccan wifey cuts his toenails and everything.
JIHAD	That's butters.
ASIF	My guy was hitting up Shagadir every year.
JIHAD	You want a maid then, Siffy?
RASHID	Yeah, Sif, you're in the sunken place for Asian boys.
	RASHID *and* JIHAD *laugh.* ASIF *looks irritated.*
	We're just playing, *yara*.
ASIF	*Bhenchoda.*
	RASHID *puts his arm round* ASIF. ASIF *shrugs him off.*
	Nah, nah, all I'm saying is it'd be nice to have a little bit of help now that I'm working.
JIHAD	Do you feel like that's a cultural thing? About expectations being put on you?
ASIF	J, what's with these questions?
JIHAD	Just to get a sense of where you stand on –
ASIF	– Pass the pipe, Mr BBC.
	ASIF *takes the shisha pipe from* JIHAD.
	I just don't get how I'm meant to prove myself, bruv. I don't even think uni is the answer, look at Jihad, my man is still jobless.
JIHAD	I'm actually starting something pretty big, bruv. So yeah.

ASIF *checks himself for a second.*

ASIF   My bad, J. I didn't mean –

RASHID   – You still going for that promotion at
                Lucketts?

ASIF   Bruv, if this manager gives me the chance innit.
                These lot don't wanna reward loyalty do they?

RASHID   Loyalty is dead in this *dunya*.

JIHAD   Go on, tell us what happened then. Who
                broke your heart this time?

                JIHAD *has a look to see if his phone is still
                recording.*

ASIF   Met this girl on the app innit. Arab girl.

RASHID   Jeez, Arab yeah? Is that you yeah.

ASIF   Jordanian, thank God coz –

JIHAD   – Focus on the story, Sif.

RASHID   Don't censor him, J, press freedom and that.
                Go on, Siffy.

ASIF   Yeah so anyway, it was clear we both fancied
                each other.

RASHID   So far, so good.

                JIHAD *takes the shisha pipe back.*

ASIF   We got different hobbies too, she likes
                protesting and that.

RASHID   Where's she from?

ASIF   I told you, Jordanian.

RASHID   Nah, I mean, where in London?

ASIF   East London, and I'm from West. Truly
                Romeo and Juliet shit. We were breaking
                barriers. Breaking the East-West divide.

JIHAD	Sounds promising.
RASHID	Innit, what's the problem, Siffy? Why aren't you two engaged then? Half your deen and that.
ASIF	Rash, I'm getting there. This new generation get distracted too quickly.
JIHAD	Siffy –
RASHID	ASIF, continue, bruv!!

ASIF *takes back the pipe much to* JIHAD's *bemusement.*

ASIF	Alright cool, right right right, so I asked for her digits and we move off the app. We got more comfortable, my lines got a bit more saucy.
JIHAD	I really want to know what a saucy line is for you, Sif, but I'm scared it'll scar me for life.
ASIF	Bro. You know how it is innit. Late-night texting. Maybe we got a bit ahead of ourselves too. Arguing about doing *dakbe* and *bhangra* at the wedding.

And we got through that awkward bit. Like –
Y'know –
Like, understandably –
– not everyone is on premarital tings innit.

RASHID	Good to clarify that shit.

RASHID *spuds* ASIF. JIHAD *takes back the shisha pipe from* ASIF.

ASIF	So far so good innit. So we decided to progress things.
RASHID	Did you meet in person then or what?
ASIF	Yeah, we met.
JIHAD	And?

RASHID	Where'd you go? How was it?
ASIF	She came west and we went Nandos. I thought great. This is comfortable innit.
JIHAD	(*To* RASHID.) Where'd you take Hanifa on your first date?
RASHID	Dixy Chicken. I paid obviously. I remember finishing all her chips and she wiped the chilli off my chin. That's when I knew innit.

ASIF *does a fake 'Awww'.* JIHAD *laughs.*

I was fifteen, bruv. How'd it go then, Sif?

ASIF	It was chill. She got a wrap. I thought, great, that's wifey material. Ordering half-chicken is a red flag innit.

Awkward pause.

RASHID	Bruv, what?
JIHAD	That's out of pocket, Sif.
ASIF	Alright yeah, sorry yeah, you're right. Anyway, the convo was flowing. We talked life. She talked about wanting to travel everywhere. I talked about Mum and Afz.
	Oh yeah and we were saying how important it is to start getting more on *deen*, as a couple innit. Like not hardcore religious but religious enough so we can enter *Jannah*.

RASHID *is nodding.*

RASHID	Five pillars. Major key.

RASHID *spuds* ASIF.

JIHAD	Can we stop spudding each other for stupid shit please? How did it go wrong then?
ASIF	I'm getting there, J. We hadn't really talked about work. Obviously, I told her I'm trying to be area manager for Lucketts. Told her

	about all the different types of dickheads who rent luxury cars. Bare man walking round like penguins pretending to own the gaff.
JIHAD	What's her family like?
ASIF	She said they were comfortable. She lives at home. But part of me. I dunno. Bro, just felt a bit odd.
RASHID	What do you mean?
ASIF	You know, my situation isn't exactly stable. It's just me, Mum and Afzal, and that's a lifestyle change.
RASHID	Siffy, why you getting in your head for? Look at me and Hani. She don't care about that shit.
JIHAD	Rash is right, that stuff is minor, Sif. What happened after that?
ASIF	I asked her about her job yeah.

ASIF *takes the shisha pipe off* JIHAD.

	She said she got a training contract straight after uni. At twenty-two I thought? She must be really smart to be advancing that quick. She talked about her first few months at this firm Smithson and Jones. And, bruv, I've seen *Suits,* I know what these *goreh* will be doing. You seen what that Harvey Specter does?
JIHAD	He's a fictional character, Sif.
ASIF	I do know that, J.
JIHAD	What do her parents do?
ASIF	Her dad's a lawyer and her mum's a doctor.
RASHID	Jeez, *Mashallah.*
ASIF	Yeah exactly. *Mashallah.* Then look at us, look at me. It ain't so *Mashallah* then is it.

JIHAD	Asif, *different* can work, bro. She's Arab and that shouldn't be an obstacle.
ASIF	I know, but I tried to imagine our families meeting, tried really hard and that shit gave me anxiety. I think she could tell something was off. So she tried to change subject but I just kept asking her about her law firm. And then I asked her if she 'always wants to work' in future innit.

Pause.

RASHID	That's bit intense for a first date, bro.
JIHAD	Yeah, Siffy, can't lie, that's a lot.
ASIF	She sorta ghosted me after that innit.

Pause.

Fuck love anyway.

RASHID *puts his hand on* ASIF's *shoulder*

RASHID	She weren't the right one for you, *yara*.

Scene Three

A few weeks later at Chunkyz Shisha Lounge.

JIHAD	You look stressed, bro?
ASIF	Every week, new drama.
JIHAD	Work shit?
ASIF	I got ninety-nine problems but work ain't one.
JIHAD	Afz?

ASIF *nods.*

What now?

ASIF	The dickhead got into another fight.
JIHAD	With who?
ASIF	Chota's little brother.
JIHAD	How though?
ASIF	Fuck knows? Something about disrespecting him on the pitch.
JIHAD	He alright?
ASIF	Who, Afz? Not a scratch on him. Chota's little brother got a broken nose though.
JIHAD	Shit, bro.
ASIF	I was gonna drag him to theirs to apologise but now his brother is saying he's gonna get Chota to beat me up.
JIHAD	Chota's mad skinny and short innit?
ASIF	Nah, bro. Chota is built like the Asian Brock Lesnar.
JIHAD	Chota is hench? I thought Tiny was hench?
ASIF	Nah that's his oldest brother. He's *actually* tiny innit.
JIHAD	But Chota is big?
ASIF	Yes, bro. That's what I said innit. The man is a tank.
JIHAD	Tiny drives a Porsche right? What does he do again?
ASIF	Sells Hajj packages.
JIHAD	And his cousin runs that erm, that gentleman's club?
ASIF	That strip club yeah. But now he's thinking of starting a new Halal burger spot. Burger Bros.

JIHAD	Creative.
ASIF	I'm gonna need Rash to settle this thing with Chota, J, calm it all down.
JIHAD	He knows them innit? I'm sure he'll sort it.
ASIF	Rash the UN peacekeeper. How's that *Pipe Dreams* thing going anyway, J?
JIHAD	It's going alright. Yeah. I mean even the CEO is liking the idea but –
ASIF	– That's sick, bro.
JIHAD	But, it's kind of like, it's maybe not exactly what I'd make right, but I thought if I get my name out there, I can make whatever I like.
ASIF	Why wouldn't you make exactly what you want though?
	RASHID *enters with a triumphant swagger.*
RASHID	Yes yes, lads.
	JIHAD *gets a phone call.*
JIHAD	Hold on, I gotta take this, boys.
RASHID	Man like Riz Lateef.
ASIF	Riz Lateef is a woman, Rash.
RASHID	'Man like' has no gender, bro.
JIHAD	You lot, please shut up.
	(Gorah *voice.*) Hi, lovely hearing from you, Fiona.
	Mike likes the new direction? Wow. Yeah sure. Interviewees, right. More of that? Okay. Coffee sounds wonderful. A few notes, yes absolutely fine. HA. Okay. Fantastic.

RASHID	(*Imitating* JIHAD.) 'Fantastic.'
	RASHID *is cracking up*.
ASIF	My guy has got the *gorah* laugh down to a tee.
JIHAD	What? I was speaking normally?
RASHID	Not gonna lie yeah, you sounded like my second cousin's white husband Ian from Cheshire.
	Imagine yeah, his wife Bushra wanted him to get a circumcision when he converted.
	My man was forty.
ASIF	Ya Allah.
RASHID	That North Face got teefed!
ASIF	The summer look.
JIHAD	Yo. I feel sick, Rash.
ASIF	What you saying, Rash?
RASHID	You lot. I got some news yeah. BIG NEWS.
JIHAD	Go on.
RASHID	Guess who's gonna be Asian businessman of the year?
JIHAD	Lakshmi Mittal?
ASIF	Chunky?
	RASHID *points at himself*.
	YOOO. Henchism?
	RASHID *nods*.
	It's happening, bruv.
RASHID	It's happening, brothers.
	JIHAD *and* ASIF *embrace* RASHID.
ASIF	*Hamdulilah*, Rash, you deserve this.

JIHAD	Incredible, my bro. You got the loan?
RASHID	I made it work, J.
ASIF	Who's the partner?
RASHID	Haz.
JIHAD	Haz?
RASHID	He likes the concept innit.
JIHAD	Haz? Rash, you sure about this yeah?
RASHID	Everything is coming together, J. I'm thinking to even propose to Hani.
ASIF	*Yara*, this is beautiful news all round.
JIHAD	For real, Rash.
ASIF	We need to celebrate.
RASHID	I'm with you lot, what else is there to celebrate? Yo actually, let me show you lot the kind of workouts I'd do.
ASIF	I've had too much biryani, Rash.
RASHID	Bro, shut up and stand. You as well, J.

ASIF *and* JIHAD *stand.*

Basically, what you don't wanna do is for your arms to be straight when doing them. They should be at an angle. Like this yeah.

RASHID *does twenty press-ups with ease.*

Look at the form, boys.

ASIF	(*To* JIHAD.) Perky bum. Like a Filet-O-Fish bun.

JIHAD *laughs.*

JIHAD	Filet-O-Fishes are soft, bro.

ASIF	See I would do that, bruv. But I do kind of like my love handles you know. Don't body-shame my *boti*.
JIHAD	*Boti* positivity.
RASHID	What you lot on about?
ASIF	Nothing. Bruv, I came here to chill, not faff about on my hands.
RASHID	You like to fap about with your hands instead innit, Sif?
	JIHAD *laughs*.
ASIF	Shut up, Rash.
RASHID	Hurry up, man, get on your knees.
ASIF	Don't tell me to get on my knees, bruv.
RASHID	Ten push-ups.
ASIF	TEN?
RASHID	Go on, Sif.
	ASIF *begrudgingly does ten press-ups*.
	TWO.
	AND THREE. FOUR.
	KEEP THAT FORM, ASIF.
	FIVE.
ASIF	Jesus –
RASHID	Is our prophet in Islam, c'mon, Asif, SIX.
	SEVEN.
	ASIF *gets up*.
	Alright good effort. J, your turn?

JIHAD	Rash, honestly, I'd love to but you know, the floor is a bit dirty and –
RASHID	Do you lot want this free consultation or not? I need to do a thorough analysis of your strengths and weaknesses, J.
ASIF	At… Chunkyz… though?
RASHID	You lot asked for it. C'mon, J.
JIHAD	Fine.

JIHAD *reluctantly does ten press-ups. Both* ASIF *and* JIHAD *are breathless.*

RASHID	Nice, J. Someone's been secretly practising.
ASIF	His… form's all… off, bruv, look at his shoulders.
RASHID	He's decent.

JIHAD *gets up.*

Come let's sit. Yo, Sif, your shoulders have come out more, my g.

JIHAD	It's his jumper.

RASHID *laughs.* ASIF *sticks a middle finger up at* JIHAD.

We're probably the only boys doing press-ups here.

RASHID	Only at Chunkyz.
JIHAD	You gonna quit Heathrow soon then?
RASHID	I'll be escaping this nine-to-five lifestyle soon *Inshallah.*
JIHAD	Soon you'll be running shit at Henchism.
ASIF	Only thing I can picture is Uncle Changez doing hip-thrusts.

ASIF *imitates an uncle doing a hip-thrust.*

JIHAD   I can't unsee that.

RASHID *laughs.*

RASHID   Only thing is, Haz was saying to widen it out innit. More profits that way so it'd be for everyone.
So, Henchism would be like body-weight training for beginners.

ASIF   It's gotta be better than Southall Better Gym. Booked a game of badminton and almost died in the changing room, bruv. The smell of *hing* and BO can kill a man.

RASHID   Air fresheners in the changing room, got you.

JIHAD   Glad you're getting this going, Rash.

RASHID   Yeah, we got a potential site now. Proper big warehouse.

ASIF   Bro, this is mad news. *Subhanallah.*

They sit.

J, start up the shisha. I brought cards innit.

JIHAD *takes his phone out and places it face down on the table. He starts up the shisha.*

ASIF *starts handing the cards out.*

JIHAD   Cool. What we playing?

ASIF   Bullshit.

They collect their cards and look at them. ASIF starts smoking. They take turns to place their cards down for a game of Bluff.

RASHID   Come let's do this! Two twos.

JIHAD   How's Afz doing anyway, Sif? Everything good? Two threes.

ASIF	Afz has made life LONG. I forgot every teenager is a little twat. One three.
RASHID	What's going on?
	JIHAD *starts recording*.
ASIF	What's not been going on?
	Getting suspended from school for shottin' weed.
	Getting into fights like with Chota's bro.
RASHID	Chota's little bro? I'll squash the beef with Chota, don't stress.
ASIF	Yeah, I might need you to, bro.
RASHID	Listen though yeah, this thing with Afz ain't a joke.
	We gotta pull him out of this early. Two fours.
JIHAD	One five.
ASIF	It could be a phase innit. Look at you now, Rash. Three fours.
	ASIF *places his cards down*. JIHAD *calls bullshit*.
JIHAD	– BULLSHIT. Don't try it, Sif. Collect your cards
	ASIF *looks annoyed*.
	ASIF *collects the cards*.
	But yeah, Rash is right, Sif. These kids don't know who they are at sixteen. They just get this constant barrage of social-media pressure. What do you expect? Two tens.
RASHID	Three Jacks. We gotta let Afz know we see him innit. And give him something to focus on, bro.

ASIF	It's all a headache. Mum works full time, so do I? I haven't got the time. One Queen.
	Mind you, it didn't help that Mum kept sending his teacher the middle-finger emoji thinking it's the pointing-up emoji.
RASHID	You know what, Afz is my little bro too. Let me chat to him. He could even help me with the gym ting.
JIHAD	One King. Why do you think Afz is doing this though, Sif?
ASIF	He's thinking, why should he focus in school when he's seeing *aapneh* run insurance scams in the ends making more in a day then you would in a few months working in retail.
JIHAD	You need to make sure he doesn't do anything that could impact his future, Sif.
ASIF	Imagine yeah, last week I clocked that he bought fake money to show off on Snapchat. My guy paid for FAKE MONEY. This new generation, man.
	Rash, it's your go.
RASHID	I feel sorry for kids these days. Three Aces.
	JIHAD *glances at his phone to make sure it's recording.*
JIHAD	Alright erm, so Rash, yeah, you see the 'young offender' stuff, you ever regret that? Like maybe it all got out of control?
ASIF	What is this, Jeremy Kyle? Two twos.
JIHAD	One three. Nah obviously you don't need to answer that.

RASHID	Two threes. Nah, I mean, I don't mind. It is what is. You grow from it. I feel sorry for him –
JIHAD	For the kid?
RASHID	Yeah obviously I was vexed back then but I feel like we're both set up to fail. We both lost… in a way. I guess he lost a little more.
JIHAD	What do you mean? Two fours. Last card.
RASHID	He killed himself.
JIHAD	Shit.
	I didn't know. What? Why?
RASHID	Whatever he did to my aunty and uncle. All the racist shit, the harassment… it was fucked. Bricks through their window. Pointing a BB gun at my aunt.
	Course the *harami* police did nothing. Even told my uncle not to call him a thug. But you know what I clocked. That kid was taught all that shit.
	In the end, he was just broken. Toxic cycle innit.
	They stop playing Bluff for a few moments.
JIHAD	How old was he?
RASHID	Sixteen.
JIHAD	Damn.
ASIF	You remember how Mrs Clifford found out you went Pen when we got back to school. One five. Rash, it's you.
RASHID	Two sixes. Will never forget that.
JIHAD	I don't remember this, boys.
ASIF	Yeah, J, I told our class he was on an extended Duke of Edinburgh to cover Rash.

But when Mrs Clifford found out, she baited him out to the entire school.

'I'd expect better behaviour from a man who went prison.' Proper racist *shaytan* she was. One seven.

JIHAD   But do you not reckon we're our own worst enemy, Sif? One seven. Don't you lot think sometimes we – sometimes we play the victim? I dunno? This blame game isn't helping us.

ASIF   Bullshit.

JIHAD   What?

ASIF   It ain't one seven. Pick up your cards, J.

JIHAD picks up his cards, it is two sevens and a three.

JIHAD   We can't always be blameless.

RASHID   What?

JIHAD   Like facts are facts, certain things we do can be backwards.

ASIF   It's nothing to do with backwards, bro. The system is rigged.

RASHID   He's right, J.

JIHAD   I don't disagree... but we gotta keep it real too. Sif, you said it yourself, bro.

ASIF   What did I say?

JIHAD   About Afz being influenced. *Aapneh* running scams. Doing dodgy shit. All kids have to look up to is that. I don't blame Afz but sometimes I reckon we're our own worst enemies.

Like Rash, them uncles at the mosque talking about boxing being *haram*. Why we gotta be so... you know... extra? Sometimes I think we brought that *pind* mentality here with us.

ASIF   – Bruv, no one blames all the *goreh* for all the
               dodgy shit they do. No one blames their
               culture.

JIHAD   We can't be victims all the time, Sif.

ASIF   Who's a victim, bro? I call it how I see it.

JIHAD   How do you see Asian grooming gangs then?
               Or ISIS?

RASHID   I'd rather be a Jihadi than a paedo, bruv.

               JIHAD *and* ASIF *look at* RASHID. *There is
               an awkward silence.*

               What? If you forced me to choose at gunpoint
               innit.

ASIF   Rash, that's not what he's asking.

               Jihad, are you fucking serious right now?
               Do you go round pubs asking white people
               what they think of Jimmy Savile?

JIHAD   No need to get smarmy, bruv. Yes sometimes
               the media will dig us out. But if we don't talk
               about this shit, who will? We need to ask
               ourselves difficult questions. Facts are facts.

ASIF   You want us to be subservient yeah?

               ASIF *puts on a posh accent.*

               Yes, Mr White Man *Gorah*, sir. I'll move out
               your way, sir.

               ASIF *stands and salutes.*

               May I get you chai-tea, sir.

JIHAD   That's… that's not… what I'm saying though.
               I'm obviously not that guy, Sif.

ASIF   Sorry to break it to you, but they are gonna
               call us whatever they like, whether *we* give
               them an excuse or not.

JIHAD	Who is?
ASIF	These dickhead journalists.
	JIHAD *stops recording*.
JIHAD	What, you think I'm gonna be another one of them dickhead journalists then, Asif?
	RASHID *attempts to smoke the shisha but nothing comes out*.
	Pause.
RASHID	Bruv, the coal is gone. Nothing coming outta this.
ASIF	Nah, it's not what I'm saying.
JIHAD	You don't understand the industry.
	Pause.
	You have to build a reputation as an objective journalist otherwise you'll get nowhere.
ASIF	Build your rep? With who, J?
JIHAD	Not with you clearly, 'cause you've never believed in me anyway.
ASIF	You don't think I back you, bruv, is that what you really think?
RASHID	Yo, relax.
	JIHAD *pauses*.
JIHAD	I've always been on the outside with you lot.
RASHID	What you talking about, J? Speak from the heart innit.
ASIF	Outside of what exactly?
JIHAD	You lot don't always tell me shit. I'm always finding out after. I'm always out of the loop.
ASIF	I'm baffled.

JIHAD	It's like you lot don't trust me.
ASIF	Bruv, you ain't always been there. We didn't hear from you when you went uni for three years.
JIHAD	I was studying, Sif.
ASIF	Yeah, you're out the picture and now, suddenly wanna hang after ages?
JIHAD	What are you saying exactly?

Pause.

ASIF	If we were actually trying to keep you on the outside, you'd know about it.

Pause.

RASHID	I think what Sif is tryna say, J, is, why we gonna bother you about some petty shit when we know you're on to better things.

RASHID *puts his hand on* JIHAD's *arm.*

We got mad love for you, J. And we're both super-proud innit.

RASHID *looks at* ASIF.

Innit?

ASIF *nods. There is still a palpable tension in the air.*

Aight, drama over. You lot besties again yeah?

JIHAD	Leave it out, Rash.
ASIF	Allow it, man.

RASHID *smiles.*

Scene Four

JIHAD, RASHID *and* ASIF *at Chunkyz Shisha Lounge.*
A slither of mist.

RASHID	The queue at *Jummah*, bro. Gets longer every week.
ASIF	Went round the block innit. Aslam from Al-Madinah tried to skip it. He got called out by this Arab uncle yeah, and then this uncle pulled the 'no English, no English' card.
RASHID	No better feeling than praying outside in the ends.
ASIF	Don't ever pray behind Shahid the butcher.
RASHID	What happened now?
ASIF	Proper juts his bum out when he gets up from *sujud*. Arches it out like an Insta baddie but obviously, we're all praying *namaz*.
RASHID	Flaunting his back off.
ASIF	And then gets up really quick to stand, like a ninja. You know me, I'm slow and steady. So it was like a perfect connection when I got up.
	Clarted me in the head.
	RASHID *and* JIHAD *laugh.*
	It's not funny, felt like I was concussed.
RASHID	Pathan power innit. He lost his little brother you know.
ASIF	*Subhanallah*, bro. Car accident yeah?
	RASHID *nods.*
RASHID	Immy lost his dad too. Too many people passing.

JIHAD turns to look at both of them. ASIF does a dua.

ASIF   You ever walk past someone and just do a little *dua* for them?

RASHID   Nah?

ASIF   You pray that Allah looks after them too.

RASHID smiles.

RASHID   You're a real gem, *yara*.

ASIF takes the shisha pipe, but nothing seems to be coming out.

ASIF   I learnt it from this elder yeah. He'd walk around, bro. With no motive except visiting people yeah. Muslim or non-Muslim. He heard the cockney hardware store owner had cancer, he was there. That crazy aunty with pram and no baby rolling through ends, he stands there chatting to her. Proper soul-to-soul connections.

Subhanallah.

No rush. No agenda or nothing.

The recording flickers. Malfunction.

RASHID speaks but nothing comes out. ASIF speaks but nothing comes out.

ASIF and RASHID leave. JIHAD panics.

JIHAD   Yo, Rash.
Yo, Sif. Where have you gone?
Boys? It's me.
Don't go.

RASHID re-enters as MIKE.

RASHID/MIKE   You've done a great job.

ASIF re-enters.

ASIF   Chunkyz. You know what I think about
                      Chunkyz.

RASHID/MIKE Don't be afraid, Ji-Had.

ASIF   Chunkyz is home. Banging shisha and no
                      weird vibes from other people looking at you
                      and shit.

RASHID/MIKE Making them anonymous would defeat the
                      purpose.

ASIF   Proper racist *shaytan* she was.

                      ASIF *exits*.

RASHID/MIKE It's now or never.
                      Ji-Had. Don't make me say it again.

                      Blue mist surrounds JIHAD. JIHAD'*s voice
                      changes.*

JIHAD   Years of work. Years of sacrifice.

RASHID/MIKE We're excited you'll be narrating this, Ji-Had.

JIHAD   I don't know what to say.

RASHID/MIKE Be grateful.

                      RASHID/MIKE *exits*.

JIHAD   It'll be on radio? My voice?

                      It's a d-d-dream. Truly.

                      Once I do this, I can make anything I like.
                      Rewrite the narrative. Rewrite the narrat–

                      The sound of laughter from a dinner party.
                      JIHAD *has lost his voice but someone is
                      speaking for him.*

VOICE   Truth.

                      He gets on his knees to search for his voice.

                      Power.

What is good?

Canned laughter.

What is bad?

Canned laughter.

What is evil?

Where are you going?

Sink or float?
Sink or float?
Sink or float, Jihad?
Ji-Had?

JIHAD *holds his throat.*

The blue mist begins to dissipate and JIHAD
comes back to his senses, he sits back down.

The recording starts.

JIHAD   *Shisha Boys: The Pipe, Protest and Perversion.*
This is Ji-Had Hussain for Ajami Media.

ACT THREE

Scene One

A few months later at Chunkyz Shisha Lounge. ASIF, RASHID and JIHAD are celebrating the launch of his audio-documentary. Raf-Saperra's 'N.L.S.' is blaring out of the speakers.

RASHID gets up and starts dancing.

RASHID	CHUNKY. I BEG YOU TURN IT UP.
	ASIF gets up and starts singing the chorus with JIHAD. The track changes to will.i.am & Cody Wise's 'It's My Birthday' and RASHID brings sparklers and hands it to JIHAD.
JIHAD	It's not my birthday, Rash.
	RASHID and ASIF laugh.
RASHID	Oi, Chunky, sort us out with your finest bottles of *Shloer*. WHITE GRAPE, MY G.
	Oi, J, why didn't you dance with us, bruv?
JIHAD	I'm a terrible dancer.
RASHID	Today is the day, J.
RASHID	You're a fully fledged journalist innit.
JIHAD	Honestly, boys, let's just chill.
ASIF	Bruv, why wouldn't we tune in? You're the next big thing innit.
	And it took ages for Rash to convince Chunky to play it on the speakers.
JIHAD	On the speakers at Chunkyz? Are you serious? NAH. NAH. Boys. We are not doing this.

RASHID	Yes, bruv, we're serious. Everyone needs to hear this.
JIHAD	It's gonna piss everyone else off, trust me it's not a good idea –
RASHID	– Who cares, bruv, my boy is gonna be on national radio!
ASIF	J, is it gonna be your actual voice?
JIHAD	Erm.
ASIF	Like your actual voice on the airwaves yeah?
JIHAD	I-I think so, I've only heard snippets so –
ASIF	– Mad!
JIHAD	Boys, I really think we should... rethink this, man. I can just send you lot the link and we can –
ASIF	– Link shink, we're lucky Rash found the link in the first place, you've been proper stoosh about this from day.
RASHID	Own this moment, J. Hold that W.
	Come, here's the pipe.
JIHAD	I should go, bro. It's cringe hearing this out loud. I actually need to go you know. I'm heading –
	RASHID *grabs* JIHAD's *arm and forces him to sit.*
RASHID	– SIT!
ASIF	J. I want to be real with you for a second.
	I know I gave you a hard time, bro. But I want you to know how happy I am that we got one of our own repping us.
RASHID	Our boy done GOOD.

JIHAD *wriggles in his seat.*

RASHID *exits briefly and re-enters with a bottle of Shloer.*

It's party time, *yara*.

ASIF *and* RASHID *laugh.* JIHAD *is smoking the shisha pipe anxiously.*

Let's go!

ASIF   Oi, CHUNKY SAAB. Turn the music off and turn the radio on please.

RASHID *grabs* JIHAD*'s shoulder. Some demure mood music introduces the documentary. A familiar voice is heard.*

JIHAD   (*Audio.*) Mass migration has changed parts of Britain.

RASHID   What? That's you, bruv!! Madness.

ASIF   Natural radio voice, *Mashallah*.

ASIF *pats* JIHAD*'s shoulder.*

JIHAD   (*Audio.*) South Asian migration in the 1950s and sixties has changed communities and neighbourhoods in Britain from Walthamstow to Wilmslow Road. A generation on, barriers are yet to be broken down. Which even residents admit has meant deep segregation has persisted.

Shisha lounges are increasingly commonplace signs of our diverse, multicultural society in Britain, but they can also make life a misery as hubs of crime, and a sign of an increasingly insular society.

They have arrived here from the Middle East and Asia where they are long established as communal meeting places. People gather to smoke a pipe known as a hookah or galyan. Traditionally they would have used tobacco, or even opium. Here in Britain, herbal ingredients are smoked in designated areas which must be no more than fifty per cent enclosed. It's becoming increasingly popular among all sections of the community, especially young people.

JIHAD *continues to blow smoke*.

In this series, we look at what's gone wrong with second-generation South Asian men.

'Shisha Boys: The Pipe, Protest and Perversion.'

JIHAD *begins to smoke the shisha pipe with increasing speed*.

South Asian boys growing up in isolation, living at home for longer, attending segregated schools and struggling to integrate, often turn to shisha bars as a place of rest, and relief.

Some have claimed critiques of these shisha spots are subject to a 'censorship' through the guise of not disturbing the multicultural status quo. A state of affairs mirrored in the now notorious case of Rotherham grooming gangs and the Trojan Horse Scandal.

ASIF *looks bemused*.

One thing is for sure. There is no smoke without fire.

In some hidden recordings, we hear from young South Asian men speaking candidly, and what follows may shock listeners.

ASIF*'s voice begins to play in the documentary*.

ASIF   (*Audio.*) Why should he focus in school when
              he's seeing *aapneh* run insurance scams in the
              ends making more in a day then you would in
              a few months working retail.

              (*In person.*) You what?

RASHID   (*Audio.*) I'd rather be a Jihadi.

JIHAD   (*Audio.*) Some of what you hear may be
              distressing. These young South Asian men
              include twenty-five-year-old Asif, who is an
              assistant manager of a car-rental company and
              twenty-four-year-old Rashid, who works
              part-time as a baggage handler at Heathrow
              despite having a troubled past, having been
              previously jailed for GBH for attacking
              a young boy in Luton.

ASIF   Chunky, turn this shit off.

JIHAD   (*Audio.*) Both these men speak to us frankly
              about their own insecurities and
              vulnerabilities as practising Muslims in
              modern British society.

              JIHAD*'s voice trails off.*

              ASIF *looks incensed.* RASHID *gets up.*

              JIHAD *puts the shisha pipe to one side.*
              Blackout. We hear the ending of the audio
              documentary.

              Critics of these kinds of insular hubs have
              claimed they promote an ethos imbued with
              extremist thought where misogyny and a
              deplorable attitude toward non-Muslims are
              shared on a regular basis.

              Some have gone as far as to suggest that this
              creeping Islamisation of Britain's social
              spaces should result in far more scrutiny on
              shisha lounges across the country.

> A space like Chunkyz Shisha Lounge is sadly
> an embodiment of this. A broken and
> culturally divided Great Britain.

Scene Two

RASHID *is running a training session for aunties in the local park.*

RASHID *is shadow-boxing.*

RASHID   One, two, three, four. Let's go!
              KEEP GOING. Don't stop.
              Shagufta Aunty, I see you, killing them.
              Lameesa, yep, imagine this is your
              mother-in-law.
              Pow.
              Eyes up here, Neelam Aunty. Alright.
              TEN MORE SECONDS! Final flurry, shine
              that shoe.

              RASHID *leads one last flurry of punches.*

              TEN, NINE, EIGHT, SEVEN, SIX, FIVE,
              FOUR,
              THREE, TWO.
              AND.
              ONE.

              RASHID *breathes in.*

              AND BREATHE. Wow, you lot kill me.

              As he staggers away, ASIF *walks on stage
              from the other side.*

              I will see you next week, ladies.

              Neelam Aunty, please stop texting my personal
              phone, I'm not sure who gave it to you.

ASIF	YES, RASH.

ASIF and RASHID spud each other.

Keeping all the local aunties fit yeah?

RASHID	It's a start, bro.
ASIF	One thing's for sure, you got Neelam Aunty looking less like a *Ladoo* and more like a snack. Phwoar.

RASHID laughs. He removes his gloves and wipes his face with a towel.

RASHID	She is thirty years older than you, Siffy.
ASIF	And single! I'm single. Let's make it work.

RASHID laughs.

Alright, we training or what?

RASHID	Come.

RASHID puts on the pads.

Put them on.

RASHID hands ASIF the boxing gloves.

ASIF	But this is got Aunty-Ji hand sweat in it?
RASHID	Hurry up, Sif. Let's go, straight into it.
ASIF	Hold on, lemme stretch innit.

ASIF starts doing hip rotations.

RASHID	Is that for Neelam Aunty yeah?
ASIF	Nah, helps with the glutemus maximus innit.
RASHID	You done? Alright, come on.

They start boxing.

I'm ready. One two.
One two.

And again, Siffy.
Nice.

Let's switch it up.

ASIF *is out of breath.*

ASIF   Lactic acid build up. Too much *salaan* last
                night.

RASHID   One, two. One two.

                Pause.

                So erm, Haz pulled out.

ASIF   Bro, I thought that was still on track?

RASHID   He just ghosted, bro. It is what it is. Come on,
                let's go.
                Three, four.
                Three four.
                Keep going.

ASIF   Bun that guy, bruv. These lot got no moral
                compass. He's gonna regret it 'cause the idea
                is sick!

                Pause.

                Anyway, what's the latest on the wedding
                plans, Rash?

RASHID   Yeah, Hani, she's been on it. Like organising
                shit. Booking that little hall above Karachi
                Express for the *nikah*. Three, four.

                Pause.

                She deserves a lot more.

ASIF   None of that shit matters, bro.
                She gets that.
                Otherwise this wouldn't be happening.
                Rash, you're getting married to your soul mate.

                And you'll make it work, *yara*.

RASHID	*Inshallah*. Come on, stop distracting me, one two.
	Good form, Sif.
ASIF	Serious?
RASHID	Solid jab, bro. Keep going, come on.
	Yo, you er, heard from Jihad recently. He's still calling me, Sif.
	ASIF *stops boxing.*
ASIF	So what? He called me too. Aired him every time. Don't tell me you answered him, Rash. Bruv?
RASHID	I didn't answer. But I feel like I should respond.
ASIF	Why? It's done, bro.
RASHID	I've had some time to think innit. And I wanna hear what he has to say.
ASIF	What do you wanna know, Rash?
	Pause.
	You know how long it took me to find new work, bro?
RASHID	I know, Sif, I know.
ASIF	– No you don't know.
	Work suspension. Official enquiry. 'Sorry, Asif, we'll have to let you go, we can't endorse that kinda language', from the same fucking manager who once called a customer a 'towel head' and 'curry muncher'.
	Applying job, after job, after job. Four months, bro. With all my experience?
RASHID	Siffy, I know what you been going through. Trust me, I do. But I need to make sense of this.

ASIF	Makes sense of what? That my mum is in a constant state of depression 'cause of this? That Afz left home still shotting and I can't do anything in my power to stop him. I was jobless. So what am I meant to say to him?
	'Trust the system, stay in school, lil bro.'
	ASIF *looks around suspiciously.*
RASHID	Why you looking around?
ASIF	Feel like I've been speaking too loudly.
	Pause.
RASHID	Siffy, chill, it's just me. We're cool here, bro.
	RASHID *pauses.*
	This can't be how this shit ends. It's a lifelong friendship, Sif. Do you not wanna look him in the eye? Do you not want the truth?
ASIF	The truth? He turned us into clowns, bruv.
RASHID	Sif, best believe I got questions for him too.
ASIF	Milano. Huqqa Hub. Bandit. Damascus Lounge. And Chunkyz.
RASHID	Yeah?
ASIF	ALL CLOSED, RASH.
RASHID	I know, bro. I know.
ASIF	Do you? Do you really though, 'cause I'm not getting the sense that you do, cuz?
RASHID	I get it. I'm saying we can't control that.
ASIF	I can't be jarred then?
RASHID	Course you can, but practically what you and I can do, is get closure. Direct from the source.
ASIF	I'm not meeting him. *Kasmeh* I'm not. You know what Chunky told me?

RASHID	He got shut down yeah?
ASIF	The fuckers raided his yard like it's an ISIS hideout. Bare feds. They thought he does some weekly Taliban link-up on Thursdays.
RASHID	Fuck. His actual yard?
ASIF	Do you get it now, bruv?
RASHID	I always got it, Sif.
ASIF	*Shukr Hamdulilah.*
RASHID	But I still think it'd be good for us. I don't wanna regret not finding out why.
ASIF	You know he got nominated for some big award yeah?

Pause.

Why do I feel like, if we do meet him, you're gonna accept anything he says? Like he could do one of them 'I'm going on Hajj, forgive me pls' WhatsApp forwards. And you'd be cool with it.

| RASHID | I'm not. I'm not cool with anything that happened. Sif, listen to me. |

RASHID *puts his hand on* ASIF*'s shoulder.* ASIF *shrugs him off.*

| ASIF | – Hold on, where is it? |
| RASHID | What you doing? |

ASIF *takes his phone out and reads an article out loud.*

| ASIF | Here we go, 'Rashid, the ex-convict mentioned in the *Shisha Boys* documentary is an example of this worrying trend. A whole swathe of young, South Asian Muslim men prone to violence and vulnerable to radicalisation.' |

> RASHID*'s eyes light up in anger. He tries to grab the phone.*

RASHID   Where's that from?

> ASIF *moves the phone away from* RASHID*'s hands.*

ASIF   Not so zen now yeah?

RASHID   This shit ain't funny, bro. If my name's out there like that it could hurt the business.

ASIF   Do you finally get it?

RASHID   I asked you a fucking question, Sif. WHERE IS THAT FROM?

ASIF   You see how deep this thing goes yeah, Rash?

RASHID   SIF.

ASIF   It ain't a joke to you now is it.

RASHID   ASIF, I FUCKING ASKED YOU A QUESTION.

> RASHID *grabs* ASIF.

Show me where you fucking read that.

ASIF   Yo, alright alright, man, calm down. Calm down. Let me go.

> ASIF *hands his phone to* RASHID. RASHID *lets* ASIF *go and frantically looks at the phone.*

RASHID   Who the fuck is writing this shit?

Al-fred Harms-worth? Who is he?

Bruv, do you fucking have any clue about the shit I've been dealing with. After Heathrow, they kept my phone. Screened all my shit. I got fucking humiliated, bruv. If I wasn't on some terrorist list, I'm definitely on one now. And

now Haz has pulled out and now I got you
waving shit in my face, there's a line you don't
fucking cross.

ASIF *looks upset, like he's on the verge of
tears.* RASHID *turns to him.*

RASHID *looks guilty.*

Yo, Siffy.

ASIF *sniffles.*

I'm sorry, man. That got out of hand.

Bro?

ASIF	I'm good, bruv. I'm fine innit.
RASHID	Bro. I'm sorry.
ASIF	Don't worry innit. I didn't know about all that. That's fucked up.
RASHID	That was really out of order. I lost it.
	Come, give us a hug.
ASIF	Nah, bruv, I'm good, I'm good.
	ASIF *is about to cry.*
RASHID	Look at me yeah. Look at me. I always got your back, Sif. Whatever happens, man.
	I love you, *yara.*
	ASIF *wipes his face and composes himself.*
ASIF	Love you, bro.

Scene Three

Jihad's bedroom. A podcast-style set-up with JIHAD *in the middle and empty chairs beside him.*

JIHAD	Alright cool. First question. What's your favourite shisha flavour?
ASIF	(*Audio.*) Super Nova mixed with Fallen Star and White Cake. Savacco.
RASHID	(*Audio.*) I don't even smoke you know.
JIHAD	Chunky?
CHUNKY	(*Audio.*) Blue Mist, brother.
JIHAD	How you been, Chunky?
CHUNKY	(*Audio.*) Areh *Bund Vajgaya*. I come out of *mott da kou*. *Bhenchod* council officer fining. *Kanjus* bastards sharing one pipe between four. This *Maachod* Dishy Rishy tax tax tax. Where does it go, brother?
RASHID	(*Audio.*) I miss Chunkyz, man.
ASIF	(*Audio.*) I get you, bro.
RASHID	(*Audio.*) We still find a way though.
JIHAD	What do you mean?
ASIF	(*Audio.*) They can never fully shut us down.
RASHID	(*Audio.*) No one's got that power over us.
CHUNKY	(*Audio.*) Except Allah.
ASIF	(*Audio.*) There's no place like Chunkyz though.
JIHAD	Why?
ASIF	(*Audio.*) Bro? You know why?
RASHID	(*Audio.*) For the vibes, *yara*. For the vibes.
ASIF	(*Audio.*) Chunkyz. You know what I think about Chunkyz.

	Chunkyz was home. Banging shisha and no weird vibes from other people looking at you and shit.
JIHAD	Boys. That whole *Shisha Boys* stuff. I need you to know that –
RASHID	– J. It's bless now. What's done is done.
ASIF	Don't worry, bro. It's all good.
JIHAD	No, no, I need you to know that –
RASHID	– At least we still got each other, yeah?
JIHAD	And where are you all hanging out now? What's the new spot?

No answer.

Boys? Rash? Sif? Hello?

Mist takes over. The echoey murmurs of the Qalandar.

Scene Four

RASHID *and* ASIF *in their local park. A few weeks later.*

JIHAD *enters.*

RASHID	Salaam, Jihad.
	JIHAD *goes into greet* RASHID. RASHID *steps back, spuds* JIHAD *coldly.*
JIHAD	Salaam, boys.
	JIHAD *looks at* ASIF, *a moment of tense eye contact.*
	Salaam, Asif.

ASIF   Yeah, Walaykumsalaam, Jihad.

                  Pause.

                  Saw you got nominated for that award. Mr
                  BBC yeah?

JIHAD   I really didn't think... it would become
                  massive like that.

ASIF   You didn't think about much did you. Just
                  yourself then?

RASHID   Sif?

                  Pause.

JIHAD   Do you lot know... do you know what
                  happened to Chunky.

ASIF   Why d'you wanna know?

JIHAD   – To-to see how he's doing.

                  ASIF *laughs.*

RASHID   Chunky moved to Dubai.

                  Pause.

                  You got anything to say, J?

JIHAD   I-I-I didn't want it to happen the way it did –

                  I tried calling you lot, tried texting, I even
                  called your mum, Sif –

ASIF   – You got what you needed.

JIHAD   It... didn't even feel like my voice. Like I get
                  it was my voice but it didn't –

ASIF   – It was some AI ting yeah?

JIHAD   I didn't write it, it wasn't my idea to go down
                  that road –

ASIF   – They put a gun to your head?

RASHID   Sif, let the guy speak innit.

                ASIF *walks away in frustration*.

JIHAD   I erm, I felt like… It's like they, kinda twisted
                my idea and-and… it turned into something
                else. I'm not gonna lie and say, I wasn't like
                d-d-drawn into it yeah? But –

RASHID   – J. That doesn't explain what you did, yeah?

JIHAD   You're right. Yeah. It was fucked and I thought
                it was like. Like, this could be a stepping stone.

ASIF   Is that what we are to you?

JIHAD   No, no, Sif, not that you would be but…
                That's not what I meant, I-I never thought it
                would be as bad as it was. I didn't think it
                through.

RASHID   Why did you call me and Sif, J?

JIHAD   'Cause I wanna find a way to make this right
                and –

RASHID   – You gonna say any of this shit publicly
                then?

                Silence.

ASIF   There's your answer, Rash.

JIHAD   No, obviously, I really do love you lot –

RASHID   – Jihad. You know what real love looks like.
                It's you taking responsibility for what you did.

                Pause.

                After I got out of young offenders and heard
                what that kid did to himself. I thought I must
                be a shit person. It took me a long time to
                clock that I needed to work on myself yeah?

                – But now I got *suqoon* in my heart 'cause
                I know who I am. God knows my intentions.

If you can't show out for us, even now, then you're just a coward, bruv.

JIHAD   Rash, I –

RASHID   – Own it, J. Like I said, I always knew you'd blow up.

JIHAD pauses, then stutters.

JIHAD   I –

ASIF   When's that award ceremony then?

JIHAD   It's… next month.

ASIF   Good for you, bruv. Take it all in yeah?

                 (*To* RASHID.) Come, shall we bounce?

RASHID   Come. Good luck with it all, Jihad. I mean that, yeah.

                 JIHAD *and* RASHID *shake hands.* ASIF *doesn't.*

                 RASHID *and* ASIF *exit.*

Scene Five

Awards show.

VOICE-OVER   Audio documentary bring us stories of real people and in doing so open us up to the important issues facing us today and tomorrow.

                 This year's winning documentary is an absorbing and poignant portal into the lives of young, Pakistani men and the attitudes that define their adolescence. Unveiling new insights into shisha lounges, segregated communities and the risk to wider society.

ADA's best audio documentary award goes too…

…Ajami Media's *Shisha Boys: Pipe, Protest and Perversion*!

Canned applause. JIHAD *enters with a crumpled piece of paper.*

JIHAD   I um. I'd like to start by –

Canned applause.

– I umm. I want to –

Pause.

I don't really have the words. But I have this poem, and it will tell you about the other side. The other side that… this documentary didn't show.

And um, I want to dedicate to Asif and Rashid:

'White Applause' by Jamal Mehmood.

Young boys in their crisp white *jubbas* (they
    will call them *thawbs*, but do not speak
    Arabic)
March in a city centre – apologising, to
    piercing white applause.

They paint quite the picture in their small
    frames, uniformly white *topis* hiding
    black hair,
Oiled the night before by loving mothers,
    with no sign of white applause;

Their bodies covered by cloth stitched by
    their aunts to the tune of a brutal white
    pittance,
Cloaked in employment figures, avoidable
    disasters – and white applause.

News cameras project the image into my
home – maybe pushing salt into my
wounds
Works like ointment for theirs, at home, as
they sit back, giving white applause.

If only I could tell you, bro, what it looked
like to see myself that way,
To have them think you were safe. For the
good ones, there is white applause.

A Nick Hern Book

Blue Mist first published as a paperback original in Great Britain in 2023 by Nick Hern Books Limited, The Glasshouse, 49a Goldhawk Road, London W12 8QP, in association with the Royal Court Theatre, London

Blue Mist © 2023 Mohamed-Zain Dada

Mohamed-Zain Dada has asserted his right to be identified as the author of this work

'White Applause' © 2023 Jamal Mehmood, first published by Hajar Press as 'White Applause in the North of England' in *The Leaf of the Neem Tree* © 2021 Jamal Mehmood

Cover photography by Mathushaa Sagthidas

Designed and typeset by Nick Hern Books, London
Printed in Great Britain by Mimeo Ltd, Huntingdon, Cambridgeshire PE29 6XX

A CIP catalogue record for this book is available from the British Library

ISBN   978 1 83904 288 1

www.nickhernbooks.co.uk/environmental-policy

www.nickhernbooks.co.uk

facebook.com/nickhernbooks

twitter.com/nickhernbooks